D0530383

Landmark

ADVANCED | Workbook WITH KEY

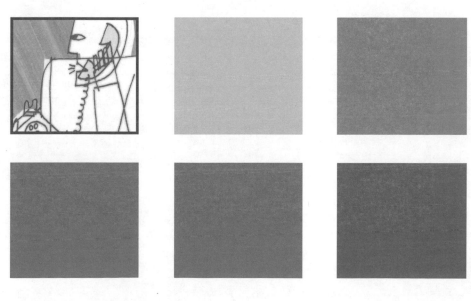

Barbara Stewart

OXFORD

The eighteen units in this Workbook will help you
- consolidate your grammar
- increase your vocabulary
- develop your listening and reading skills
- improve your pronunciation and your understanding of features of spoken English.

Each unit has four parts.

Language focus

This section contains a variety of exercises which give you extra practice of the language points you have studied in the Student's Book. Many units have practice based on authentic texts, where you can see particular language points in real contexts.

There are also recorded exercises on the Student's Cassette, which give you oral practice of key grammatical structures.

Vocabulary focus

This section revises and extends topic vocabulary, collocation, and phrasal verbs from the Student's Book.

Vocabulary expansion

This section uses an authentic text to provide the starting point for the study of new vocabulary, particularly idioms, word-building, and synonyms. The texts, which are thematically linked with topics from the Student's Book, come from sources ranging from newspaper and magazine articles to extracts from novels. As well as helping you develop your vocabulary knowledge, this section also gives you the opportunity to improve your reading skills.

Listening

This section has a variety of recordings in a variety of accents. All the recordings are authentic and are between one and three minutes long, approximately. There are exercises to prepare you for each recording, to guide you towards understanding, and to help with new or difficult vocabulary. The **Follow up** section focuses on a particular feature of spoken English or has extended vocabulary work.

Tapescripts of the recordings can be found at the back of the Workbook.

How to use this Workbook: a step-by-step guide

This Workbook can be used alongside the Student's Book as a source of supplementary classroom material. It can also be used for self-study; all the activities have been designed so they can be used by people working on their own. We suggest you read through the information in this introduction before you begin and refer back to it as you work through the different sections of the Workbook. We hope you will find the Study tips useful.

Language focus

The exercises in this section give you extra practice of the language studied in the Student's Book. We suggest that you do the Workbook exercises after you have studied the language point in class. Don't forget to refer to the **Language commentary** in the Student's Book.

Study tips
- Do the exercises in the order in which they appear when there is more than one exercise practising one particular language point, as these are graded from easier to more difficult.
- Focus on one language point at a time rather than doing all the exercises in one go. This will help keep things clearer in your mind.
- Keep yourself motivated and challenge yourself by varying how you do the language exercises. You could, for example, read the relevant section in the Language commentary in the Student's Book first, then do the related exercises in the Workbook. Or you could test yourself to see how much you know by doing the exercises in the Workbook first, and then looking at the Language commentary if you have made mistakes.
- If you are less sure of a language point, write the answer on a piece of paper instead of in your Workbook. That way, if you make mistakes, you can try the exercise again a week later.

Recorded exercises

Each unit contains an exercise marked ⌒ which is recorded on the Student's Cassette. These exercises allow you to listen to and repeat sentences containing important language points you have studied in the Workbook. As well as providing useful oral practice of grammatical structures, these exercises also help you to improve your pronunciation.

Study tips
- Do the recorded exercises the day after you have done the written exercises to see what you can remember. Then come back and try them again a few days later.
- Try to imitate the speakers on the recordings as closely as possible. Concentrate on copying their intonation, rhythm, and connected speech.
- Don't forget, you can listen to the exercises when you are doing other things, for example, when you're in the car or working out in the gym.

Vocabulary focus

This section is designed to consolidate and extend your vocabulary. We suggest that you do the exercises after you have looked at the particular vocabulary sections in class.

Study tips

- Review all your vocabulary regularly. Test yourself or work with a friend and test each other. Make it more fun by doing it by e-mail.

Vocabulary expansion

The main aim of this section is to introduce new vocabulary through a text which is related to a topic in the Student's Book unit. These exercises can be done at any time and in any order, as long as you read the text first. You might like to read the text in this section one day and do the related vocabulary exercises at another time.

As the texts are authentic, you may find that several of the exercises include completely unfamiliar vocabulary. There may, for example, be phrasal verbs or idioms you have never met before, and you may be asked to decide whether definitions of new words or idioms are true or false. In exercises like this you should make an intelligent guess or use a dictionary before checking your answers. These are important skills which will help to make you an autonomous learner, more able to study independently and effectively.

Study tips

- Buy an English–English dictionary if you don't already have one. There are many good dictionaries available, for example, the *Oxford Advanced Learner's Dictionary*.
- To find the meaning of an idiom in a dictionary look up the first full word (verb, noun, or adjective, not article or preposition) contained in the idiom, e.g.
  try your hand at something.
  Look up *try* in your dictionary and you will find

  IDM to do sth such as an activity or sport for the first time

  However, in some cases, especially if the first full word is a very common one (*go, do, make, good, bad, etc*), you may have to look up the second full word in the idiom, e.g.
  make light work of something
  Look up *light* and you will find

  IDM to do sth quickly and with little effort

- Be selective. You cannot learn *all* the words and phrases at once, so choose the vocabulary which seems most useful or most interesting and transfer it to a vocabulary notebook, file, index cards, or your computer.
- Don't simply record the word. You need to know how to pronounce it and what other words collocate with it too, e.g.
  kid (n): / kɪd / (informal) child or young person
  She's just a kid.
  (vb)   (informal) to deceive often in a playful way
  I was only kidding when I said I was rich.
  You're kidding yourself if you think it'll be easy.

- Read as much and as often as you can (the Internet is a good source of reading material), but don't overuse dictionaries. If you stop and use your dictionary every time you meet an unfamiliar word, you will find it harder to understand and enjoy what you are reading. Try to guess the meaning of words and idioms from their context, then use your dictionary at the end to check your guesses.

Listening

The activities in this section are designed to improve your listening skills, extend your vocabulary, and improve your understanding of some of the features of spoken English. The exercises can be done at any time but we suggest that you do them in order.

Most listenings have a pre-listening activity. You may be asked, for example, to predict what you are going to hear. This helps you prepare for listening by building up a mental picture.

All the listenings have two activities to do while you are listening. The first of these helps you check the gist or the general meaning; the second checks more detailed understanding.

There is also a vocabulary exercise, which checks your understanding of important vocabulary in the recordings.

The last activity, **Follow up**, focuses either on interesting vocabulary in the recording or on a particular feature of spoken English, such as unpronounced sounds, weak forms, or stressed syllables. These are awareness-raising exercises so don't worry if you get some of the answers wrong.

Study tips

- Don't expect to understand everything the first time you play the recording. Just listen straight through and try to get the gist. In real life, very often general comprehension of the main points is all that is required.
- Don't be tempted to look at the tapescript until you have done the second listening exercise. If you can't answer the questions after the second hearing, you can always listen again.
- Do make use of the tapescripts *after* you have finished the listening exercises. They allow you to look at the language used by the speakers at *your own speed*. You can see why you found a particular section difficult (e.g. unknown vocabulary, unfamiliar pronunciation, etc). You can either read them and then listen again without looking, or read and listen at the same time. As you listen pay attention to the features of natural spoken English.
- Try to do the vocabulary activity without using a dictionary. This helps you develop the important skill of guessing the meaning of unknown words from their context.

A final word of advice. When using a Workbook, the best rule is little and often. That way you're more likely to remember what you've studied. But however you decide to use it, we hope you enjoy it.

1

Language focus

Discourse markers SB p.7

1 Choose the correct discourse marker from the highlighted pair.

1 Antonio Gaudí, born in Spain in 1852, is considered to be one of the greatest architects of his time. For example / In particular, he is known for his work *La Sagrada Familia*, which, it is hoped, will actually / eventually be finished.

2 Walt Disney, the American animator and film producer, made his name with the creation of many cartoon characters. Incidentally / On top of that, Mickey Mouse was originally called 'Mortimer'.

3 Whether you like him or not, and in particular / to be honest I don't, Michael Jackson is an important figure in the history of popular music. At first / In addition he performed with his four older brothers in the pop group The Jackson Five, before later going solo.

4 Many people consider Cary Grant (1904–1986) to be one of the best film actors ever. Even so / Anyway, he was never awarded an Oscar for a specific performance.

5 Muhammad Ali is one of the most admired figures in the history of boxing. Actually / To start with, the former world heavyweight boxer fought under the name Cassius Clay. Then, in 1964, after converting to Islam, he changed his name.

6 Few men rank alongside Charlie Chaplin in the history of the cinema. He was a brilliant actor and a distinguished director. To sum up / By the way, he was a genius.

2 Complete these sentences with a word or phrase from this list. Use each item once only.

apparently   by the way   foolishly   in retrospect
personally   seriously   understandably   up to a point

1 Amy was injured in the accident. ...., she hadn't been wearing her seat-belt.

2 ...., I should never have married Steve. Deep down I knew he wasn't the settling-down type.

3 ...., although girls outperform boys at school, boys have a much better general knowledge.

4 Theresa's parents aren't coming to the wedding. Theresa is, ..., very upset.

5 A Eric doesn't think we should spend money we haven't got on a new car. I agree with him ...., but we're spending so much on repair bills for our old one.

B ...., I agree with Eric. Buying a new car is a waste of money. But it doesn't really matter what I think, does it?

6 A I've applied for a job as a flight attendant. Do you think I stand a chance?

B I think you'd make an excellent flight attendant. You love ordering people about and you're always spilling drinks. You'd be brilliant! No, ..., I think you stand a very good chance.

7 Don't worry if you can't make it on Friday. We can get together some other time. ...., have you heard about Owen? Apparently he's handed in his notice.

all, both, either, neither, none SB p.11

3 Complete this dialogue with *all, both, either, neither,* or *none.*

A What's wrong? You look stressed out!

B I am. Frank and I can't decide where to go on holiday or what kind of holiday to go on for that matter.

A What about Spain? Sandy beaches, lots of sun.

B .... **1** of us is very keen on a beach holiday. I burn really easily and Frank gets bored sitting in the sun.

A What about a city break, then?

B Frank isn't mad about sightseeing and, to be honest, I'm not .... **2**.

A Is there anything .... **3** of you like?

B I suppose we do .... **4** like holidays where you do things – activity holidays.

A Why don't you go on one of those then?

B Yes, but which one? There are so many and they .... **5** look interesting.

A What about diving in the Red Sea? That sounds fun.

B Yes, but I'm not a very good swimmer. .... **6** is Frank, come to that.

A What about something creative, like painting?

B I thought of that, but I've looked at loads of brochures and .... **7** of them have painting holidays. Where are you and George going on holiday?

A We haven't decided yet .... **8**. Hey, why don't we .... **9** go somewhere together? If we can find something that we .... **10** like doing, of course.

B I think that might be a slight problem, don't you?

4 Rewrite these sentences using the word in bold.

1 Alex can't cook and she can't sew either.
neither
....

2 Tim likes Italian food. So do Bobby and Lily.
all
....

3 Quentin is selfish and bad-tempered too.
both
....

4 John and Sandra hate ironing. So do I.
none
....

5 Bethany and Grace can speak a little German.
both
....

🎧 **1.1** Listen, check, and repeat.

Vocabulary focus

-isms SB p.10

1 **a** Complete the crossword using the clues in these sentences.

Across

3 A ...... deliberately damages or destroys property.

6 A ...... is admired for his or her courage.

8 A ...... has a negative outlook on life.

9 A ...... believes that people only do things for their own advantage.

Down

1 A ...... believes that some races are superior to others.

2 A person who is addicted to alcohol is an ......

4 A ...... judges the quality of films, books, etc.

5 A ...... believes that women should have the same rights and opportunities as men.

7 An ...... looks on the bright side of life.

b Complete this list by forming a noun which ends in *-ism* from each of the answers to 1a.

1 *racism*   6 ....

2 ....   7 ....

3 ....   8 ....

4 ....   9 ....

5 ....

c Complete these sentences with a word from 1a or 1b in an appropriate form.

1 I'm too much of a ………… to believe that he won't want something in return for his help.

2 ………… had senselessly broken branches and uprooted plants.

3 Apparently, a positive attitude to illness can aid recovery, so ………… must have a distinct advantage.

4 The ………… movement has brought about changes in the English language. Many references to gender have been removed.

5 The reward for ………… was given to a 12-year-old boy who put his own life at risk to save someone from drowning.

6 Would you read my manuscript? Any ………… would be welcome as long as it's constructive.

Describing people: metaphors and idioms `SB p.12`

2 Complete the metaphors in these sentences with an appropriate word from this list.

---
bag   bright   cool   couch   loose   lost   pain   waste

1 Martin does nothing but watch telly and stuff his face with pizza all day. He's nothing but a ………… potato.

2 My little brother's always getting on my nerves. He's a real ………… in the neck.

3 I think Maria should put some weight on. There's nothing to her. She's just a ………… of bones.

4 I don't know what Victoria sees in him. Personally, I think he's a complete ………… of space.

5 Sophie often puts her foot in it and says the wrong thing. She's a bit of a ………… cannon.

6 Which ………… spark suggested we visit the castle today? It's closed on Sundays!

7 You're wasting your time trying to reform him. He's a ………… cause. Once a gambler, always a gambler!

8 A Have you noticed how Harry always stays calm, even in a crisis?

   B Yes, he's quite a ………… customer, isn't he? I don't think I've ever seen him get ruffled.

Vocabulary expansion

1 Read the article about the Hollywood film director Alfred Hitchcock and decide whether these statements about him are True or False.

1 Hitchcock was a shy man. ☐

2 He has had a great influence on modern cinema. ☐

Hitchcock's
legacy

With a total of over fifty films to his credit, Alfred Hitchcock has left an indelible mark on the film industry and, even now, more than twenty years after his death, he is still one of cinema's most prominent figures.

5 An accomplished self-publicist – Hitchcock's face appeared on posters and trailers for his movies and he regularly made cameo appearances in the films he directed – Hitchcock would have revelled in the attention
10 he's getting today.

But the image that most people have of 'Hitch' – that he was a bit of a joker, an amusingly eccentric English gentleman – is
15 not the whole story. Those who knew him best describe him as cold, insecure, and uncharitable.

Hitchcock's films achieved mass popularity because they were consistently entertaining; they also provided the
20 template for many modern genres. *The 39 Steps*, with its mix of humour and adventure, paved the way for the Bond films, which combined the same ingredients. *Psycho* and *The Birds* almost defined the modern horror movie.

Hitchcock himself played down his achievements
25 describing his movies as 'slices of cake – delicious perhaps, but insubstantial'. But such comments are somewhat inaccurate. Few would dispute that whatever genre he was working in, Hitchcock brought to it his own particular inimitable style.

Adjectival suffixes: *-ible* and *-able*

1.2 *indelible*   1.30 *inimitable*

2 a Match these nouns with the adjectives they collocate with.

behaviour   breakdown   damage   decision   food
goods   impression   manner   ~~mark~~   product   style

indelible   *mark*   ....

(in)edible   ....

inimitable   ....

(ir)responsible   ....

irreversible   ....

irrevocable   ....

marketable   ....

objectionable   ....

b Check your answers then complete these sentences with an appropriate adjective + noun combination from 2a.

1 I find his .... quite .... He is just so rude.

2 With the success of groups like Take That and The Backstreet Boys in the 1990s, boy bands became very ....

3 Sunbathing can do .... to your skin, ageing it prematurely.

4 The service in the restaurant was appalling and the .... was scarcely ....

5 The company chairman said that the .... to close 100 branches was .... It had been taken after careful deliberation.

6 Marlon Brando played the part of Vito Corleone in his own ....

Adverbs

1.13 *amusingly eccentric*   1.19 *consistently entertaining*

3 Try to choose the correct adverb from the highlighted pair in these sentences.

1 His toothache was so fiercely / excruciatingly painful that he found it impossible to concentrate.

2 It's one of the best plays I've ever seen. The acting was worryingly / positively brilliant!

3 Advertising is a dog-eat-dog, internationally / fiercely competitive business.

4 Damon drove excruciatingly / worryingly fast along the narrow country roads.

5 Wales' positively / internationally famous singer, Tom Jones, started his singing career in the 1960s.

Listening

You are going to hear Katie talking about her great-aunt, who has been a great influence on her.

1 🎧 **1.2** Listen to the recording once and decide which sentence best describes Katie's feelings for her.

▶ **Note** multiple sclerosis is a disease of the nervous system.

a She feels very close to her great-aunt.

b She admires her great-aunt.

c She feels sorry for her great-aunt.

2 Match these highlighted words and phrases from the recording with their meanings.

1 *She has* outlived *the average expectancy …*

2 *She has a* wicked *sense of humour …*

3 *She's an* inspiring *person …*

4 *She is never* self-pitying *…*

a ☐ mischievous; wanting to shock

b ☐ making one feel one can achieve anything

c ☐ feeling sorry for oneself

d ☐ lived longer than

3 🎧 **1.2** Listen again and decide whether these statements are True or False.

1 Auntie Frances got multiple sclerosis when she was in her mid-twenties. ☐

2 People with multiple sclerosis don't normally live to an old age. ☐

3 Auntie Frances has been in a residential home for most of her adult life. ☐

4 Frances loves having visitors. ☐

5 Frances rarely complains about being ill. ☐

Follow up: correcting wrong information

4 a 🎧 **1.3** Listen to how Katie corrects wrong information. Underline the words she stresses most.

She's sixty-nine now em in fact no, she's seventy-nine.

b Check your answers to 4a. Then correct any wrong information in these sentences. Underline the syllables that should be stressed.

1 Katie's aunt's called Auntie Mary.

No, she's called Auntie Frances.

2 Frances got multiple sclerosis when she was twenty-three.

3 She stays in a retirement home.

4 She's been there for the last fifteen years.

5 She's got a poor sense of humour.

2

Language focus

The conditional SB p.15

1 Correct any mistakes in the verb forms in these sentences.

1 If I'd bought a new car instead of an old one, I wouldn't have to spend so much money on repairs.

2 Take out full insurance cover, or you'll be in trouble if you had been involved in an accident.

3 If I am still working as a sales rep, I would still be driving over 500 km a day.

4 Get one scratch on the car and it's the last time I would lend it to you.

5 I won't be here now if the crash had been more serious.

6 I think I would be a more confident driver now if I had learnt to drive when I was eighteen.

2 Rewrite the underlined parts of these sentences using the words in bold.

1 Nowadays, <u>if you don't own a mobile phone</u>, you are seen as old-fashioned and out of touch.

unless

unless you own a mobile phone

2 I would use mine more often <u>if it weren't so expensive</u>.

but for

....

3 <u>Unless you've got an old-fashioned phone</u>, you can send written messages to people.

as long as

....

4 Although there is still controversy over the safety of cellular phones, most users believe they don't do any harm <u>unless they are overused</u>.

provided that

....

5 <u>Without one</u>, how would you keep in touch with people?

Supposing

....

3 Complete these sentences by putting the verb in brackets in the correct form.

1 If I .... (not know) how to use a computer, I wouldn't have got the job.

2 If I agreed to buy you a mobile phone, ... you .... (promise) not to run up a huge phone bill?

3 If she'd had her phone on her when her car broke down, she .... (be able) to phone the breakdown services.

4 If my computer hadn't crashed, I wouldn't have had to redo all my work, and I .... (sit) at home watching television now.

5 If you .... (not have) a mobile phone these days, you're in the minority.

6 If I had a computer, I .... (do) all my shopping on the Internet.

7 If you .... (be) worried that a file might be contaminated, don't download it.

8 If you .... (make) a point of backing up your work, you needn't worry about anything going wrong.

🎧 2.1 **Listen, check, and repeat.**

4 Complete this extract from a short story by putting the verbs in brackets in the correct form.

Long Live the Queen

A
S SHE CAME BACK ROUND THE HOUSE, she saw a woman in the garden next door. This was a neat and tidy garden with flowers and a lawn. The woman was in her 50s, white-haired, slim, wearing a twin-set.*

'One of the cats ran out in front of my car,' Anna said. 'I'm afraid it's dead.'

'Oh dear.'

'I've put the – body, the body on the coal shed. Do you know when they'll be back?'

'It's just her,' the woman said. 'It's just her on her own.'

'Oh, well. I've written a note for her. With my name and address.'

The woman was giving her an odd look. 'You're very honest. Most would just have driven on. You don't have to report running over a cat, you know. It's not the same as a dog.'

'I couldn't have just gone on.'

'If I .... **1** (be) you, I .... **2** (tear up) that note. You can leave it to me. I'll tell her I saw you.'

'I've already put it through the door,' said Anna.

She said goodbye to the woman and got back into her car. She was on her way to her parents' house, where she would be staying for the next two weeks. Anna had a flat on the other side of the town but had promised to look after her parents' house

while they were away on holiday, and – it now seemed a curious irony – her parents' cat.

If her journey .... **3** (go) according to plan, if she .... **4** (not delay) for half an hour by the accident and the cat's death, she .... **5** (be) in time to see her mother and father before they left for the airport. But when she got there they had gone. On the hall table was a note for her in her mother's hand to say that they had had to leave, the cat had been fed and there was a cold roast chicken in the fridge for Anna's supper. The cat would probably like some too, to comfort it for missing them.

Anna did not think her mother's cat, a huge fluffy creature called Griselda, was capable of missing anyone. She could not believe it had affections. Anna knew that it was absurd to call an animal selfish, an animal naturally put its survival first, yet she thought of Griselda as deeply, intensely, callously selfish. At night it lay on their bed and if they .... **6** (move), it .... **7** (dig) its long, sharp claws through the bedclothes into their legs.

Anna's mother did not like hearing Griselda referred to as 'it'. She corrected Anna and stroked Griselda's head. Griselda, who purred a lot when recently fed and ensconced among cushions, always stopped purring at the touch of a human hand. This would have amused Anna if she hadn't seen that her mother seemed hurt by it, withdrew her hand and gave an unhappy little laugh.

Ruth Rendell

* **A twin-set** is a woman's matching jersey and cardigan. Twin sets were commonly worn by middle-class, middle-aged women with conservative views

Emphasis SB p.17

5 Complete B's replies in these mini-dialogues. Use appropriate auxiliaries to give them emphasis.

1 A You don't know what you're talking about.

  B I ....*do know*.......... what I'm talking about.

2 A You wouldn't mind if my parents came to stay for a few weeks, would you darling?

  B Yes, I ....

3 A Rachel didn't like the film, did you Rachel?

  B I .... it. I just thought it was a bit long.

4 A Anthony said he couldn't come because he was ill, but I think he just didn't want to.

  B He .... actually. His mother told me he had flu.

5 A Stephen doesn't love me any more.

  B He .... you.

6 Rewrite these sentences in a less emphatic way.

1 She's a lovely girl, Deirdre.

  ....

2 He said you weren't interested, Kieran did.

  ....

3 I definitely will be there!

  ....

4 It was too long, the book was, to my way of thinking.

  ....

5 They're very nice to drive, Ferraris are.

  ....

6 I really am fed up with your attitude!

  ....

Vocabulary focus

make and *do* SB p.16

1 a Complete the expressions in these sentences with a word or phrase from this list.

a good turn   a mountain out of a molehill   a night of it
do   good   my day   the most of   very well for himself

1 It made .... when I heard that Terry had got the sack. I can't stand that man.

2 I'd love to buy a new dress for the party but I really can't afford to spend money on clothes right now. I'll just have to make .... with what I've got.

3 Simon's a great guy. He did me .... the other day. He typed up that report for me.

4 I've only got a week's holiday but I intend to make .... the time I've got and cram in as much as I can.

5 I know you've got a strict deadline but why don't you come out with us tonight? A break will do you ....

6 Peter has done ...., hasn't he? A degree from Oxford and now a well-paid job in the City.

7 I think you're making .... It's only a small problem.

8 We were just going to come straight home after the theatre but then we decided we might as well make ...., so we're going to go out for dinner afterwards.

b Check your answers then match the expressions from 1a with their definitions.

1 exaggerate a problem   ....
2 spend the whole night and not just part of it doing something   ....
3 do somebody a favour   ....
4 be beneficial   ....
5 become successful or wealthy   ....
6 use to the best advantage   ....
7 make very happy   ....
8 manage with what you have   ....

Vocabulary expansion

1 Read this article and decide which piece of advice you think is the most useful.

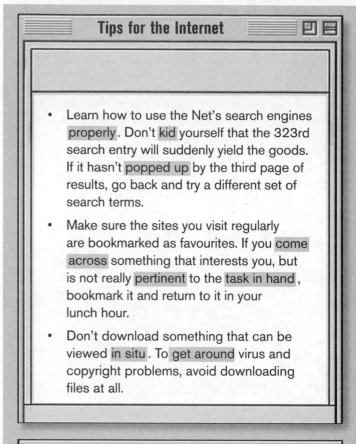

Tips for the Internet

- Learn how to use the Net's search engines properly. Don't kid yourself that the 323rd search entry will suddenly yield the goods. If it hasn't popped up by the third page of results, go back and try a different set of search terms.

- Make sure the sites you visit regularly are bookmarked as favourites. If you come across something that interests you, but is not really pertinent to the task in hand, bookmark it and return to it in your lunch hour.

- Don't download something that can be viewed in situ. To get around virus and copyright problems, avoid downloading files at all.

Tips for e-mail

- Don't risk confusing your reader by missing out punctuation or capital letters. Pause before you send every message and check who you're sending it to. Read it again. Ask yourself if your tone is too informal.

- Get permission to e-mail clients.

- Remove anything in a message that might cause offence or confusion. Make it as short as possible.

- Colour code incoming messages in order of priority – so the boss can be red, your brother blue.

- If someone in the office is sending you too many messages, why not walk over to talk to them instead?

Nick Paton-Walsh, The Guardian

2 a The article is written in a mixture of formal and informal language. Match the highlighted words in the text with their formal or informal equivalents in this table.

Formal	Informal		Informal	Formal
1 *in situ*	where it is		5 *properly*	correctly
2	the job you are doing at the moment		6	encounter
			7	overcome
3	offend or confuse		8	appeared
4	to do with		9	deceive

b Complete these sentences with an appropriate formal or informal word or phrase from your table.

1 Magda says she's on a diet but she's just .... herself. I've just seen her eating a packet of crisps.

2 The problem can be .... if the candidate's interest in the company is publicly declared.

3 The photocopier isn't working .... We'll need to get someone in to have a look at it.

4 Could you please keep to the agenda? What you have just said is not .... to the point under discussion.

5 A I saw Malcolm at a classical music concert on Friday and Julie says she saw him at a rock concert on Saturday.

B He .... all over the place, doesn't he?

Listening

You are going to hear the continuation of the short story you read on page 11 about Anna and the cat.

1 🎧 **2.2** Listen to part 1 of the recording and decide which of these statements best expresses how Anna felt about the accident.

a She felt it had been her fault.

b She couldn't stop thinking about it.

c She soon put it out of her mind.

2 🎧 **2.2** How do you think the story will continue? Listen to part 2 and find out what happens next.

3 🎧 **2.2** Read the following sentences. Then listen to part 2 again and decide whether they are True or False.

1 ☐ Richard was a close friend of Anna's.

2 ☐ Anna answered the phone because she thought it was Richard.

3 ☐ Anna thought the woman wouldn't be too upset at the cat's death.

4 ☐ They were cut off before they had finished talking.

4 Match the highlighted words from the recording with their meanings.

1 ☐ *Discussion was useless and so was* recrimination.

2 ☐ *It had been some* consolation *to know that the woman had so many cats …*

3 ☐ *… losing one would be less of a* blow.

4 ☐ *I think you should* make amends.

5 ☐ *Anna was very* taken aback.

a sudden bad shock

b compensate somebody for a mistake, insult, or injury

c be shocked or surprised

d an accusation in response to an accusation from somebody else

e comfort

Follow up: collocations

5 Which words from 4 can be used with the following groups of words?

1 bitter; angry; pointless ..... *recrimination* .....

2 .... by somebody's rudeness; by a suggestion

3 a shattering; terrible ....

4 no; some; small; scant ....

3

Language focus

wish SB p.21

1 Choose the correct highlighted alternative in these sentences.

1 Don't you wish everyone in the world speaks / spoke the same language?

2 I wish I had studied / studied Latin when I was at school.

3 I wish French wouldn't be / weren't such a complicated language. I'll never learn it.

4 I really wish I didn't leave / hadn't left it so late to start studying a foreign language.

5 I wish English wouldn't have / didn't have so many phrasal verbs.

2 Complete these sentences with an appropriate verb in the appropriate form.

▶ **Note** You will sometimes need to use the negative.

1 I wish you _wouldn't make_ that noise. It's really irritating!

2 I wish I .... on holiday but I can't afford it.

3 I wish I .... I'd go out with Jane tonight. I'd much rather stay at home.

4 I wish I .... you tomorrow but I've already arranged to go out with Melanie. Sorry!

5 It's absolutely freezing! I bet you wish you .... some warmer clothes with you.

6 Some people are never happy, are they? They wish they .... taller or slimmer, ... more money, and .... in California. They should count their blessings.

7 My dad's always saying to me, 'You don't know how lucky you are. I wish I .... the opportunities you have when I was your age!' It really gets on my nerves! I wish he .... going on about it.

🎧 **3.1** Listen, check, and repeat.

If only SB p.21

3 Correct any mistakes in the verb forms in these sentences.

1 If only he had the sense to wear a hat, he wouldn't have got sunstroke.

2 If only the weather wouldn't be so changeable.

3 If only they can predict the weather more accurately.

4 Oh no, it's going to rain. If only I'd listened to the weather forecast!

5 If only the sun will come out!

6 If only I had enough money to buy an island in the sun.

Other ways of expressing wishes SB p.21

4 Rewrite these sentences using the word in bold.

1 I wish there was some way we could change the events of history, but there isn't.

unfortunately

.... we can change the events of history.

2 I wish I'd had a computer when I was a child.

pity

What .... a computer when I was a child.

3 I wish we could travel into the future.

shame

What .... travel into the future.

4 I really wish we could undo the mistakes of the past.

only

.... the mistakes of the past .... undone.

5 Please don't preserve my body after I die. I don't want to come back in the future.

grateful

I .... my body after I die.

6 I really don't want people to be cloned – ever!

hope

I .... cloned.

7 Sometimes I wish the telephone had never been invented.

sorry

I am .... invented.

Speculating and imagining SB p.23

5 Cross out the inappropriate modal verbs in these conversations.

1 A If time machines existed, would / ~~could~~ / might you choose to go back in time or forward?

 B I would / could / might not have to think twice. I would / could / might go back to Roman times.

2 A I'm thinking about accepting the teaching job. The drawback is that it would / could / might mean a reduction in salary.

 B Yes, but on the plus side you would / could / might have longer holidays.

3 A What about meeting for a drink on Friday afternoon – about four?

 B It would / could / might be difficult to get away early. The boss often calls a meeting then.

 A You would / could / might always say you had a hospital appointment.

 B I wouldn't dare. If he suspected I was lying, I would / could / might be in real trouble, that's for sure.

4 A Are you packing your swimming costume? I am.

 B I can't make up my mind. It would / could / might not be warm enough to swim.

5 A Suppose you could have any car you wanted.

 B Well then I would / could / might buy a BMW without question.

6 Complete this extract from an article about the future with *could* or *would* and an appropriate verb from this list. Sometimes both are possible.

be (X2)   change   consist   outweigh   suffer

Concern about the future is not new. A Miami University professor addressing a meeting of pilots a decade ago memorably described the airline of 2025. He claimed the crew _____ ¹ of just one pilot and a dog. The pilot's role _____ ² to feed and look after the dog. The dog's role _____ ³ to bite the pilot if he tried to touch anything.

Perhaps in the future we will be more affected by humanity's past failures than its current and future innovations. Twenty-first century environmental pollution and the melting of the polar ice caps _____ surely _____ ⁴ our lives in a dramatic negative way that _____ ⁵ the positive effects of the World Wide Web, for example.

Dr. John Gribbon, of Sussex University, believes the Arctic ice cap will be melting by 2025, pouring cold water into the north Atlantic and slowing down the flow of the Gulf Stream. While the rest of the world warms, Britain and north-west Europe _____ ⁶ from extended periods of cold weather.

Simon Reeve, Focus magazine

Vocabulary focus

Collocations: nouns and adjectives SB p.25

1 a Match an adjective from A with a noun from B to create as many combinations as possible.

A active   cultural   dominant   isolated   local   natural
negative   positive

B incident   differences   disasters   interest   outlook
position   response

b Complete these sentences with an adjective from A and a noun from B.

1 This region has suffered from a number of
   natural disasters , including last month's hurricane.

2 Students whose parents take an ....
   in their progress do better than those whose
   parents are unconcerned.

3 Although England and Scotland
   share the same language, there
   are many ....
   between the two countries:
   for example, in Scotland many
   men still wear the kilt on formal
   occasions.

4 The appeal for money, food,
   and medical supplies in the
   wake of the earthquake has
   met with a ....
   Contributions have been coming
   in from all over.

5 You need to be more optimistic.
   You won't get far with such a
   .... on life.

6 Medical experts had thought that the case of cholera
   was an .... Unfortunately,
   it turned out to be more widespread than they had
   at first believed.

7 There is a lot of .... in the project,
   which will affect everyone in the town and outlying
   regions to some degree.

8 Stirling Castle stands in a .... at the top
   of a hill.

* 550 **tons** = 541 tonnes

Vocabulary expansion

1 a Before you read this extract from a magazine article,
do you think these statements are True or False?

1 ☐ A drop of rain only consists
   of water.

2 ☐ Rainclouds are heavier than
   aeroplanes.

3 ☐ There is more water in the air than on the surface
   of the planet.

4 ☐ A ball will travel further if the air is humid than if
   the air is dry.

b Read the text and see if your answers were correct.

Did you know? – Clouds

* Each raindrop needs a minute speck of dirt to form
  around. This is called the 'condensation nucleus'. The
  commonest one is sea salt – even as far as 100 miles
  inland. Sand, specks of pollution, volcanic dust, even the
  tiny particles left by shooting stars are all to be found at   5
  the heart of raindrops.

* It takes about a million cloud droplets to make a single
  raindrop.

* A small fair weather cumulus cloud – about a kilometre
  wide and a kilometre high – is so full of water that, fluffy   10
  as it looks, it in fact weighs 550 tons* – more than a
  loaded jumbo jet.

* The warmer the air, the more moisture it can hold as
  invisible water vapour. For this reason there may be more
  water suspended in the air over a desert, than in the air   15
  over a mountain in the middle of a winter snowstorm.

* Of all the world's water, only 3% is in the air as invisible
  water vapour or as clouds. If all this water were to turn to
  rain simultaneously, it would cover the earth's surface
  with about one inch of water.   20

* Humid air is less dense than dry air. So, a ball will travel
  slightly further through the less dense air of a hot, humid
  day, than on a hot, dry day.

Savage Skies

Adjectives to describe size

1.1 *a minute speck of dirt* 1.5 *tiny particles*

2 Sort these words into two groups according to their size – small or large.

enormous   gigantic   huge   massive   microscopic
minute   tiny

small	large

Collocations: noun + *of* + noun

1.1 *A speck of dirt*

3 a Match words 1–8 with words a–h to make phrases.

1 a speck   a snow
2 a drop   b dirt
3 a flake   c sunshine
4 a gust   of   d sand
5 a ray   e lightning
6 a flash   f rain
7 a grain   g thunder
8 rumble   h wind

b Check your answers then complete these sentences with an appropriate phrase from 3a, making any necessary changes.

1 The country was suffering a drought. There hadn't been .... in three years.

2 Belinda lifts the spirits of everyone around her. She's a real ....

3 A storm was on the way. We could hear a distant ....

4 She's such a fastidious housewife. There isn't .... to be seen anywhere.

5 Thick .... fell on the windscreen and began to settle on the road, which would be impassable within hours.

Collocations: *hot* and *cold*, etc

4 a Complete the sentences with an appropriate adjective from the list.

cold   dry   hot   wet

1 After the flood all the carpets were soaking ....

2 It was a boiling .... day in August. The temperature must have been at least 40 degrees.

3 It was such a hot day that the clothes I'd hung on the line were bone .... a few hours later.

4 The food they serve is excellent and is still piping .... when it reaches your table.

5 It was obvious that Ryan had just stepped out of the shower. His hair was dripping ....

6 It was a bitterly .... day. Icicles hung from the eaves and there was snow in the air.

7 Sonia spat out the coffee. It was scalding .... and she had burnt her tongue.

8 It's freezing .... in here. Can you turn the radiator up?

b Check your answers then use the sentences above to help you to complete these definitions.

1 .... wet describes something which produces falling drops of water.

2 .... wet describes something which has absorbed liquid.

3 .... hot is negative and describes the temperature of liquids.

4 .... hot is neutral or negative and describes the weather or temperature of the environment.

5 .... hot is positive and describes the temperature of food.

6 .... cold describes the weather, the temperature of the environment, or food.

7 .... cold describes the weather.

Listening

You are going to hear Beverley and Anthony talking about how they feel about rain.

1 🎧 **3.2** Listen to the recording once and complete this table with a, b, or c.

a She/he likes it

b She/he doesn't like it

c She/he doesn't say

	Beverley	Anthony
rain in autumn		
gloomy weather		
drizzle		
thunderstorms		

2 🎧 **3.2** Listen again and put one word in each gap.

1 Beverley likes it when it rains if she is .... because it makes her feel ....

2 What Anthony really dislikes about rain in Britain is the .... and .... associated with it.

3 In Italy Anthony and his family ran around in the rain because it was .... and ....

4 The kind of rain that Beverley dislikes is .... because it makes ....

5 After a thunderstorm abroad it can become .... or ....

6 At the pop concert it rained so heavily that everyone ....

Follow up: stressed syllables

3 🎧 **3.3** Listen to this section of the recording and underline the stressed syllables. The first one is done as an example.

I don't actually em <u>mind</u> it when it rains, in fact, I quite like it sometimes, especially in em in autumn if it rains and you're you're inside and you're in a nice warm house and you can hear the rain pattering down outside or see the raindrops running down the windows makes you feel quite quite cosy em but I mean I know a lot of people get very depressed with with the rain.

4

Language focus

Narrative tenses `SB p.31`

1 Follow the instructions for each section of the story.

a Choose the correct highlighted alternative.

It was a short drive home. Bruce knew / was knowing ¹ every inch of the road, and every inch of that part of the river too. As a child he was catching / had caught ² fish there and learnt / was learning ³ to swim. Heavy rain pushed / had pushed ⁴ the river up over its banks and across the road a day or so before. Now the weather was clearer, but although the waters receded / had receded ⁵ a little, they were still fierce and fast.

Then it was happening / happened ⁶. Bruce's car skidded / was skidding ⁷ on the greasy road and went / had gone ⁸ out of control. For a split second he saw / was seeing ⁹ his house on the other side of the river before the car was turning over / turned over ¹⁰ and fell / had fallen ¹¹ into the water below.

b Two of the three highlighted verb forms are possible. Decide which verb form is not possible in each case.

His wife, Mary, had nearly finished preparing the evening meal, and wondered / was wondering / had wondered ¹ where her husband had got to. She didn't hear / wasn't hearing / hadn't heard ² the crash and was totally unaware that only a short distance away her husband was fighting for his life. If she had looked out of her kitchen window she might have seen the wheels of their car sticking up out of the river. Instead she began / was beginning / had begun ³ to feel irritated.

Down below, Bruce struggled / was struggling / had struggled ⁴ with his seat belt, but he couldn't undo it. His situation was critical. The car began / was beginning / had begun ⁵ to fill up with water and it was freezing cold.

c Put the verb in brackets into the correct form – Past simple, Past continuous, or Past perfect.

Fortunately for Bruce, his neighbour Ian Campbell
.... ¹ (hear) the crash and .... ²
(call) for an ambulance. By the time it .... ³
(arrive), Bruce .... ⁴ (manage) to get out of the car and reach the side of the river. He .... ⁵
(bleed) from a wound on his head and was shocked and dazed. But otherwise he was all right.

2 Read this account of a real-life rescue and correct any mistakes in the highlighted verb forms.

The call came through on the emergency phone, the direct link to ambulance control. It was clipped, to the point, the way they always are. A man was stung ¹ by bees in Wymondham.

It was only a ten-minute drive from the ambulance base station at Attleborough to Wymondham. On the way the crew, Steve Mortley and Dave Money, tried ² to work out the possibilities, to prepare themselves for what they might find. They were deciding ³ the most likely thing was a straightforward bee sting; somebody had panicked ⁴ and called them out, and by now everybody would be a bit embarrassed when they turned up because he wasn't needing ⁵ any treatment at all. It often happened.

Dave Money recognized the house when they had arrived ⁶, and realized he was knowing ⁷ the people involved. It was always an unsettling feeling; casualties are normally strangers.

He was first out of the ambulance. He snatched up the emergency case and ran down the side of the bungalow. He recognized Ross Wallace. He was standing ⁸ in the window, pointing urgently to the back of the house and the garden.

When he got to the corner of the building he could see Peter lying, face down, in the grass. Even from there he could see the air above his body was thick with bees. He took a step forward and had called out ⁹ to him, but there was no response. He went ¹⁰ a few more steps and called again. Now he could see bees around Peter's head and more of them swarming over his body. It looked for all the world like the scene of a film from a Hitchcock movie.

At that moment the bees turned ¹¹ on him. He wore ¹² a short-sleeved shirt. The bees were already on his arms and in his hair. It was no time for heroics. He turned and ran.

Dramatic stories of real-life rescues, Michael Buerk

999 EMERGENCY

Reported speech and reporting verbs `SB p.33`

3 Choose the correct highlighted alternative in these sentences.

1 Ben denied stealing / to steal the money.

2 Sharon insisted Mandy to come / on Mandy coming to her party.

3 Susan's father agreed on helping / to help her with her homework.

4 The doctor warned Pedro not to take / to not take the pills on an empty stomach.

5 Carmen doubted being able / that she would be able to go to the conference.

6 Eva suggested having / to have the party at her place.

7 Can I persuade you on giving / to give me a hand?

🎧 `4.1` Listen, check, and repeat.

4 Rewrite these sentences in reported speech using an appropriate verb from this list.

advise   ~~announce~~   ask   beg   decide   forbid   tell   think

1 'Listen everyone. I've got something important to tell you. Karen and I are getting married in June.'
Matt *announced that he and Karen were getting married in June.*

2 'I think I'll have the fish. Yes, I'll have the fish, please.'
Monica ....

3 'Please, please, please say you'll go out with me, Geri.'
Ewan ....

4 'If I were you, Roger, I wouldn't buy a new car until prices drop.'
Joe ....

5 'Sorry Rosa, could you repeat what you said?'
The man ....

6 'Don't worry. It'll be all right.'
Emma ....

7 'On no account are you to use the office phone for personal calls.'
My boss ....

8 'I'm sure you won't like what I'm going to suggest.'
Hannah ....

Vocabulary focus

Anger SB p.30

1 a Complete this table.

verb	adjective (to describe the effect of something)	adjective (to describe how you feel)	abstract noun
	X	angry	
annoy			
irritate			
	frustrating		
X	X		fury

b Complete these sentences using an appropriate word from 1a.

1 She was absolutely .... when she saw the scratch on her new car.

2 You should go on an ....-management course. You keep losing your temper for no reason.

3 Tapping his fingers on the table is just one of his many .... habits.

4 I get so .... when I'm stuck in a traffic jam but there's nothing you can do about it.

5 My initial .... at his late arrival turned to anger when he told me the real reason he was late.

Verb–noun collocations SB p.34

2 Complete these sentences with an appropriate noun from this list.

a business   a mile   facts   (one's) match   the bush
the deadline   the music   the rush

1 She'll have to face .... when her parents find out she's been missing school.

2 Joshua would run .... if I asked him to marry me. You wouldn't see him for dust!

3 We won't meet .... on this order unless everyone is prepared to do overtime.

4 Stop beating about .... and get to the point!

5 I always do my Christmas shopping early to beat ....

6 We'll just have to face .... We can't afford a holiday this year.

7 Alan is a good squash player but he met .... in David. David beat him easily.

8 You are bound to make mistakes if you've never run .... before. But you'll soon learn the ropes.

Vocabulary expansion

1 a Check this information about roads in Britain.

British roads

- Motorways generally link cities. They are denoted by a capital M and a number. For example, the M6 runs between Birmingham and Carlisle.
- 'A' roads are main roads connecting towns. Sometimes there are two lanes in each direction. They are denoted by a capital A and a number. For example, the A21 runs from Hastings to Sevenoaks.

b Read the report and find out how many roads were affected by the incident.

Traffic chaos as blaze shuts motorway

MOTORISTS across west Surrey suffered traffic chaos on Wednesday after a huge grass fire engulfed Lightwater Country Park.

Flames spread from the southbound carriageway of the M3 to the central reservation and eventually reached the northbound carriageway and the far bank.

Police were forced to close the motorway between junctions 3 and 4 just before 3 p.m., triggering the worst rush hour delays for many years.

Tailbacks quickly clogged key trunk roads and a host of other surrounding roads as drivers rushed to find alternative routes. The A30, A322, and A3 around Guildford all came to a standstill while a seven-mile queue hit the M3 itself between junctions 2 and 3.

Police were faced with the additional problem of dealing with a dozen broken down vehicles on the M3 and adjoining roads as engines overheated. Traffic at Stag Hill near Guildford was also held up while recovery crews moved a car which was blocking one lane of the A3 near the Little Chef restaurant. The M3 was re-opened to traffic at about 6.45 p.m.

Surrey Advertiser

2 a Match the highlighted words with these definitions.

1 place where two or more roads meet .... *junction*

2 section of a wide road intended for a single line of traffic ....

3 important main road ....

4 narrow piece of land separating traffic moving in different directions ....

5 part of a road intended for vehicles ....

6 long line of traffic that extends back from something blocking the road ....

b Choose the correct highlighted alternative in these sentences.

1 Motorways have three junctions / lanes : an inside, middle, and outside junction / lane . Dual carriageways, on the other hand, only have two.

2 The accident happened when the driver of a lorry travelling along the westbound carriageway / trunk road of the M3 lost control of his vehicle.

3 As a result of the accident there was a ten-mile tailback / lane .

4 If you leave the motorway at lane / junction 3 , there's a service station a few miles further on where you can get petrol and have something to eat.

5 The coach swerved, went through the crash barrier, crossed the trunk road / central reservation and was lucky not to collide with traffic travelling on the motorway in the opposite direction.

3 a Match the highlighted verbs in 1–3 with the meanings a–c.

1 ☐ *Tailbacks quickly clogged the trunk roads.*

If you eat too much saturated fat, your arteries will clog up.

2 ☐ *… triggering the worst rush-hour delays …*

The riots were triggered by a series of police arrests.

3 ☐ *Motorists across west Surrey suffered traffic chaos.*

The government has suffered a crushing defeat.

a experience or show the effects of something bad

b block something and prevent it working properly

c start something; be the cause of a sudden, often violent reaction

b Complete these sentences with an appropriate verb from 3a in an appropriate form.

1 Several people .... from minor injuries were taken to a nearby hospital.

2 It took us ages to get there. The roads .... with holiday traffic.

3 Certain foods, like chocolate, can .... headaches in some people.

Listening

1 🎧 **4.2** Listen to the recording once. What is the speaker describing?

a a life or death situation

b a holiday adventure

c a supernatural experience

2 🎧 **4.2** Listen again and decide whether these statements are True or False.

1 The incident happened when the speaker was on holiday. ☐

2 She saw something behind the shrub (=a low plant or bush). ☐

3 There were five people staying at the house at the time. ☐

4 Some people slept upstairs and some slept downstairs. ☐

5 Not everyone was frightened. ☐

3 Match these words from the recording with their meanings.

1 ☐ recollection   a person or thing that you cannot see but you feel is near

2 ☐ malevolent   b staying hidden especially when waiting to attack or appear

3 ☐ lurking   c remembered thing or event

4 ☐ presence   d having or showing a wish to do evil

Follow up: collocations

4 a Which words from 3 can be used with the following groups of words?

1 ghostly / eerie / constant ....

2 .... suspiciously / in the shadows

3 vivid / vague / earliest ....

4 .... person / look / smile

b Complete these sentences with an appropriate adjective and noun combination from 4a.

1 As I turned the corner into my street I saw a man .... outside my house. He looked as if he was up to no good.

2 During Arthur's long illness his wife was a .... She never left his side for a moment.

3 He turned to her with a .... on his face and said menacingly, 'I'll get even one day.'

4 Because Daniel hit his head on the steering wheel, he has only a .... of what actually happened.

5

Language focus

Opinions and suggestions SB p.37

1 a Read these situations. What advice would you give to the people concerned?

a Someone in Katherine's office has been taking money from the petty cash box. Katherine knows who it is but doesn't know if the person is stealing or just borrowing the money.

....

b One of Michael's colleagues has a lot of personal problems, which are affecting his work. Michael would like to do something to help but doesn't want to interfere.

....

c Liam's boss wants him to work this Saturday but Liam has promised his son he'd go and watch him play football then.

....

d Joanna quite unreasonably lost her temper with her colleague Peter the other day. Now Peter is ignoring her. She would like things to return to how they were.

....

e Lawrence has worked for the company for ten years but is always passed over for promotion. It's really beginning to get him down.

....

f A colleague of Lauren's keeps making sexist remarks.

....

b Complete these sentences with an appropriate word or phrase.

1 ☐ He .... always pretend he was ill.

2 ☐ I .... she reports him to her boss and gets him to deal with it.

3 ☐ I .... her to have a word with the person concerned first and find out what's really happening.

4 ☐ .... if she apologized and did something to make it up to him, like take on some of his work.

5 ☐ He .... find out what's happening – ask his boss directly and tell him he's not happy.

6 ☐ Why .... ask this person out for a drink and tell him he's a good listener if he needs one?

🎧 **5.1** **Listen, check, and repeat.**

c Look again at the situations in 1a and the advice in 1b. Match situations a–f with advice 1–6 by writing the correct letter in each box.

2 Rewrite this conversation using the words in bold.

1 I think smoking should be allowed in the workplace.

view

In .... smoking in the workplace.

2 I don't agree at all.

completely

I ....

3 You could ask your boss to set aside a smoking area.

simply

Why .... to set aside a smoking area?

4 In my opinion, people would do a lot less work if smoking were allowed.

considered

It .... people would do a lot less work if smoking were allowed.

5 I disagree.

along

I .... with that.

Inversion after negative expressions SB p.39

3 Correct any mistakes in these sentences.

1 Hardly the plane had taken off when one of the passengers got to his feet and started shouting.

2 Seldom does the pilot get involved in cabin disputes.

3 Not only was the man drunk, was he aggressive too.

4 Not once the flight attendants lost their temper with the passenger.

5 Under no circumstances is an airline obliged to carry a drunk passenger.

6 Not since my first flight anything so interesting has happened.

7 At no time the situation got out of control.

8 Never will the man be able to fly with that airline again.

4 Rewrite these sentences to make them less emphatic.

1 Rarely do gangs of boys behave well.
   Gangs of boys rarely behave well.

2 Never in her life had Caitlin felt so scared.

   ....

3 Not only did the boys shout at her, they also made rude gestures.

   ....

4 Hardly ever are young people penalized for breaking the law.

   ....

5 Rewrite these sentences to make them more emphatic.

1 You will only eradicate problems like this by punishing bad behaviour.
   Only by punishing bad behaviour will you
   eradicate problems like this.

2 Vandals should not be allowed to get away with it on any account.

   ....
   ....

3 Richard hasn't been in trouble since he was cautioned for stealing last year.

   ....
   ....

4 The police have made no arrests. They don't know who committed the crime either.

   ....
   ....

Other examples of inversion

6 Rewrite these sentences to make them more formal, beginning with *were* or *should*.

1 If you wish to make a complaint, please speak to the flight attendant in the first instance.
   Should you wish to make a complaint, please speak to the flight attendant in the first instance.

2 If the plane were diverted, how would passengers arrive at their destinations?

   ...., how would passengers arrive at their destinations?

3 If you are not happy with the service, we would be obliged if you would tell us.

   ...., we would be obliged if you would tell us.

4 If they required help with their luggage, they would ask for assistance.

   ...., they would ask for assistance.

5 If I asked to be upgraded to business class, how much would I be required to pay?

   ...., how much would I be required to pay?

6 If you require any assistance, please do not hesitate to ask.

   ...., please do not hesitate to ask.

Vocabulary focus

Three-part phrasal verbs SB p.37

1 Complete these sentences with an appropriate phrasal verb from this list in the appropriate form.

get away with   go back on   look down on   look forward to   move on to
put up with   run out of   send off for

1 As soon as I go back to work after a break I start .... the next holiday.

2 I don't know why you .... his rudeness. I would complain to someone about it.

3 As we can't seem to reach agreement on this, can we .... the next item on the agenda?

4 When the photocopier .... paper, this light flashes. It's best to fill all the drawers at the same time.

5 Ralph .... anyone who hasn't been to university. He's such a snob.

6 If Colin promises to do something, he will. He never .... his word.

7 As far as my boss is concerned, Helen can't do a thing wrong. She .... murder!

8 I saw this advertisement for a hotel chef in the paper the other day. It said anyone interested in the job should .... details.

2 a Here are some more three-part phrasal verbs. Match them with their meanings a–f. Use the context to help you.

1 A I believe Robin's come down with German measles.

   B Yes, he came out in spots the other day so we called the doctor in.

2 The medical board came down heavily on the doctor who had prescribed the wrong medicine for the patient, dismissing him on the spot.

3 There are too many patients and not enough beds. As yet no one has come up with a long-term solution to the problem.

4 The surgeon had wanted to perform the operation but he came up against a lot of opposition from the hospital board, who said it was too expensive. In the end it all comes down to money, doesn't it?

a blame and severely criticize for something ....

b suggest or think of an idea or plan ....

c catch or develop an illness ....

d have (a particular thing) as the most important factor to be considered ....

e face problems or difficulties ....

f (of the skin) develop (e.g. spots) suddenly ....

b Correct any mistakes in the three-part phrasal verbs in these sentences.

1 A I can't understand why Chloe has had her nose done. It looked all right as it was.

   B Yes, but it didn't look all right to her, which is what it comes down to in the end.

2 It's high time someone came up against an effective cold remedy.

3 The government came up against a great deal of opposition to their plans for closing a number of local hospitals.

4 Julia came down on her husband like a ton of bricks when she found out he had gambled away all their savings.

5 Jamie thinks he's coming out in flu so he's gone home.

6 Every time Sarah eats strawberries she comes down with a rash.

Health SB p.41

3 Do you think these sentences are True or False?

1 ☐ If you feel funny , someone has just made you laugh.

2 ☐ If you are off colour , you look pale.

3 ☐ If you have a bad night's sleep, you are likely to feel rough the next day.

4 ☐ If you are feeling run down , you have been involved in an accident.

5 ☐ If you feel sick , the best thing you can do is go to bed.

6 ☐ You can pick up a tummy bug if you eat contaminated food.

7 ☐ If you have a touch of flu , you have a bad dose of influenza.

8 ☐ Many people feel groggy after an anaesthetic.

Vocabulary expansion

1 Read this extract from a novel and decide whether these statements are True or False.

1 ☐ Every employee has to join the Pension Plan.

2 ☐ The author is an optimistic person.

The Edible Woman

I was just finishing a rush job when Mrs Grot of Accounting came through the door. Her business was with Mrs Bogue, but on her way out she stopped at my desk. She's a short tight woman with hair the colour of a metal refrigerator-tray.

5 'Well, Miss MacAlpin,' she grated, 'you've been with us four months now, and that means you're eligible for the Pension Plan.'

'Pension Plan?' I had been told about the Pension Plan when I joined the company but I had forgotten about it. 'Isn't it too soon for me to join the Pension Plan? I mean – don't you think I'm too young?'

10 'Well, it's just as well to start early, isn't it,' Mrs Grot said. Her eyes behind their rimless spectacles were glittering: she would relish the chance of making yet another deduction from my pay-cheque.

'I don't think I'd like to join the Pension Plan,' I said. 'Thank you anyway.'

15 'Yes, well, but it's obligatory, you see,' she said in a matter-of-fact voice.

The Edible Woman

'Obligatory? You mean even if I don't want it?'

'Yes, you see if nobody paid into it, nobody would be able to get anything out of it, would they? Now I've brought the necessary
20 documents; all you have to do is sign here.'

I signed, but after Mrs Grot had left I was suddenly quite depressed; it bothered me more than it should have. It wasn't only the feeling of being subject to rules I had no interest in and no part in making: you get adjusted to that at school. It was a kind of superstitious
25 panic about the fact that I had actually signed my name, had put my signature to a magic document which seemed to bind me to a future so far ahead I couldn't think about it. Somewhere in front of me a self was waiting, pre-formed, a self who had worked during innumerable years for Seymour Surveys and was now receiving her
30 reward. A pension. I foresaw a bleak room with a plug-in electric heater. Perhaps I would have a hearing aid, like one of my great-aunts who had never married. I would talk to myself; children would throw snowballs at me. I told myself not to be silly, the world would probably blow up between now and then; I reminded myself
35 I could walk out of there the next day and get a different job if I wanted to, but that didn't help. I thought of my signature going into a file and the file going into a cabinet and the cabinet being shut away in a vault somewhere and locked.

I welcomed the coffee break at ten-thirty. I knew I ought to have
40 skipped it and stayed to expiate my morning's lateness, but I needed the distraction.

Margaret Atwood

Formal style

2 The novel is written in a fairly formal literary style. Match the formal highlighted words in the text with their more common and less descriptive equivalents below.

1 was glad to have ....

2 glasses ....

3 greatly enjoy ....

4 make up for ....

5 many ....

6 saw in the future ....

7 tie (vb) ....

8 used ....

Adjectives and verbs to describe voices

1.5 *grated*

This verb describes Mrs Grot's voice. Here are some other adjectives and verbs used to describe people's voices.

3 a Read these definitions.

boom (vb); booming (adj):	a very loud, deep voice.
grate (vb); grating (adj):	a harsh irritating sound, like the noise car wheels make against the kerb of the pavement.
husky (adj):	sounding rough, as if the throat were dry.
soothing (adj):	having a relaxing and calming effect.
whine (vb); whining (adj):	a high-pitched, complaining voice.

b Complete the sentences with an appropriate word from 3a.

1 We could hear the colonel's .... voice long before he entered the room.

2 A Gloria has an attractive .... voice, hasn't she?

  B So do you, when you've got a sore throat!

3 Laura makes a good nurse. She has such a .... voice that people immediately feel more at ease.

4 Neville has such an unpleasant voice. It really .... on you.

Verbs like *shine*

1.11 *glittering*

4 a Look at these collocations.

glimmer:	lights seen through the mist or in the distance
glisten:	dew on grass; perspiration on someone's body
glitter:	diamonds; sunlight on snow
glow:	a lit cigarette; the embers of a fire

b Now match the verbs with their meanings.

1 ☐ glimmer
2 ☐ glisten
3 ☐ glitter
4 ☐ glow

a shine brightly (especially of wet surfaces)

b a faint unsteady light

c producing light (and heat) but with no flame

d shine brightly with small flashes of light

c Complete these sentences with an appropriate verb or noun.

1 At last the rain stopped and the sun came out. The raindrops in the grass .... in its rays.

2 It wasn't necessary to turn on the lights. We could see well enough from the .... of the fire.

3 From the aeroplane we could just make out through the clouds the .... of lights far below.

4 The harbour .... with lights from the many small boats anchored there.

Listening

You are going to hear someone giving their views on genetic engineering.

1 🎧 **5.2** Listen to the recording once and decide which is the best summary of the speaker's views.

a Genetic engineering is an exciting but worrying extension of genetic research.

b Genetic engineering is just another scientific development.

c Genetic engineering, like all scientific developments, will have both positive and negative consequences.

2 🎧 **5.2** Listen again and decide whether these statements are True or False.

1 ☐ The speaker thinks that genetic research was inevitable.

2 ☐ According to the speaker, people have thought a lot about what the implications of the research are.

3 ☐ The speaker thinks it would be a good idea for the views of religious leaders to be taken into account.

4 ☐ The speaker is neither for nor against genetic engineering.

3 Look at the tapescript on p.84 and choose the best definitions for these words and phrases.

1 *tick*
   a develop b work in the way it does c continue

2 *to get to grips*
   a deal seriously with a problem
   b discuss something in a serious way
   c think about something seriously

3 *uneasy*
   a worried b not safe or settled c complicated

4 *side-effects*
   a problems b risks c secondary consequences

Follow up: word stress

4 a Write these words from the recording in the correct box according to their stress pattern.

~~alliance~~ desirable development exciting implications inevitable input logical particularly probably scientific

●•	●••	•●•
....	....	*alliance*
	....	....

•●••	•●•••	••●•
....	....	....
....	....	....

b 🎧 **5.3** Listen and check your answers.

6

Language focus

Modal verbs: *should, ought to, must, have to, need to,* and other expressions of obligation
SB p.45

1 **Choose the correct highlighted alternative in these sentences. Tick any sentences where both alternatives are correct.**

1 You've got bags under your eyes. You ought to / should get more sleep. ✓

2 You really must / ~~need to~~ meet Robert. You've got so much in common.

3 I need to / ought to walk to work but the car's so much easier.

4 I know I must / should go to the gym but I can't be bothered.

5 You don't have to / mustn't be thin to be a model but most of them are.

6 People should / had better pay attention to what people are like, not what they look like.

7 If you want to have a clear complexion you had better/ need to drink lots of water.

8 You had better not / don't have to do strenuous exercise to keep fit. Brisk walking will do that.

9 You had better not / don't have to do exercise straight after a heavy meal. It's bad for you.

10 I have to / must get my hair cut. It's getting on my nerves.

11 Why are you getting up? You are meant to / had better stay in bed. You know what the doctor said.

12 A What do we have to do?

   B We are supposed to / ought to discuss what, if anything, we would change about our appearance.

   C We don't need to / don't have to change anything. We're all perfect!

13 You are not supposed to / meant to use the equipment in the gym until you've been shown how to use it.

🎧 **6.1** Listen, check, and repeat.

didn't need to / needn't have

2 **Correct any mistakes in the modals in these sentences.**

1 A You're early.

   B Yes, I didn't need to work late for once.

2 The sea was perfectly calm so they needn't have taken any sea-sickness pills, which was just as well as they'd forgotten to buy any.

3 What a waste of time. I didn't need to study World War II. There wasn't a question on it in the exam.

4 I needn't have taken Janet to the station. John did.

5 Thanks for the wine, but you didn't need to bring it. We've got plenty.

6 We didn't need to put any petrol in the tank. It was full.

Determiners: *some, any, every, no, all, few, a few, little, a little* SB p.47

3 **Complete these sentences with an appropriate determiner.**

1 Although .... people are born geniuses, ... child is born with a talent of .... kind.

2 A How many of the people you went to school with became famous?

   B Not many really. Only ....

3 .... three thousand artists are competing for the prize this year.

4 A Can I give you .... advice?

   B I'd be grateful for .... advice you can give me. I've got .... idea what I'm doing.

5 .... wind instruments are hard to play though it is true that ...., like the recorder, are less difficult than others.

6 .... winners will get medals and .... child will go home feeling that they have failed because .... participant will get a diploma and a prize.

7 .... is known about the author who is in the running for the Nobel Prize for Literature. Surprisingly .... critics seem to have heard of him.

8 Even if you have only .... talent, it can be nurtured.

9 .... person can succeed as long as they have .... talent and a lot of luck.

Vocabulary focus

Words and their roots SB p.48

1 Complete these sentences by making an appropriate word from the root in brackets.

1 Those .... in the crash were taken to a nearby hospital for treatment. Luckily, none of the .... were serious. (injure)

2 The film *The Beach* was, in my opinion, a disappointing .... of the novel of the same name. (adapt)

3 The police officer asked me for a .... of the man I had seen running away from the scene of the crime. (describe)

4 Politicians of all parties need to forget their differences and reach .... on this important issue. (agree)

5 There's nothing remarkable or out-of-the-ordinary about her. She's quite .... really. (describe)

6 This travel hairdryer comes with several .... for use in different parts of the world. (adapt)

7 A euphemism for a lie is a / an .... (true)

8 A There's a very .... smell coming from the fridge. (agree)

 B That's an understatement. It stinks!

9 Darren's .... talents were obvious from an early age. He could play the recorder when he was four. (art)

10 The campsite provides .... facilities only: toilets and a washroom. (base)

---

* One **foot** (ft) = 30.48 centimetres
One **inch** (in) = 2.54 centimetres
6ft 5in = 1.96 m (approx)

Vocabulary expansion

1 a Before you read this newspaper article extract about height, do you think these statements are True or False?

1 ☐ People who are tall do better in professional careers then people who aren't.

2 ☐ Very tall people live longer than averagely tall people.

b Read the article and check your answers.

Top of the class

APART FROM OBVIOUS ADVANTAGES when ordering drinks or playing water polo, is it really more desirable to be tall than short anyway? The answer is yes.

'It's better to be tall for almost all social purposes,' says Professor James
5 Tanner of London University. 'The evidence is that tall people tend to get to the top of their professions more quickly than others.'

They also tend to live longer. A programme in the 1950s showed a clear relationship between height and longevity. Height indicates 'nutritional status', explains Professor Roderick Floud. 'Height measures the effects
10 of nutritional intake of food and other forms of energy and warmth, even affection – against the demands on the diet for the body's maintenance.'

Genes play a part, but so do environmental factors. If you met three generations of a Japanese family who moved to California after the war, you would typically find granny and grandpa
15 smaller than their children, who are in turn smaller than their children, who are now virtually as tall as other Californians.

Absence of disease and American diets are reckoned the key factors here.

But the great era of human growth is coming to an end, Professor Tanner says. In the next generation or two, populations in the developed world will probably have reached their maximum height.

And the height / longevity advantage starts to reverse once you get above 6ft 5in* or so. 'For every extra inch, subtract a couple of years off the life expectancy,' says Philip Heinricy, founder of The Tall Person's Club. 'When you get to about 6ft 6in, you appreciate that we are nothing more than a series of levers and joints which can wear out pretty quickly.'

Peter Kingston, The Guardian

Nouns with *take*

1.10 *intake*

2 a Choose the correct highlighted alternative in these sentences.

1 The doctor has ordered him to reduce his salt intake / take-up .

2 Reports of a military takeover / take-off have been confirmed.

3 The company reports a 75% uptake / take-up of its share offer.

4 That impersonator does a brilliant take-off / takeover of the American President.

5 I don't feel like cooking tonight. Let's get a / an intake / takeaway .

b Check your answers then complete these sentences with an appropriate word from 2a.

1 Do you fancy going to a restaurant or shall we get a ....?

2 The GVQ bank has confirmed reports of a hostile .... by the Midshire Bank.

3 There has been a 100% .... of voluntary redundancy so no further staff cuts will be necessary.

4 You need to cut down your caffeine .... if you're having problems sleeping.

Nouns and expressions with *turn*

1.15 *in turn*

3 Choose the best answer. Sometimes more than one is possible.

1 If there is a turnaround in a company's fortunes, does the company
a make a lot more money?
b make a lot less money?

2 If John, Julie, and Alison take turns to ride a bicycle, who will ride the bicycle after John?
a Julie
b Alison
c Either Julie or Alison

3 If the government promises to reduce taxation and then does a complete turnabout does it
a increase taxation?
b reduce taxation?
c keep taxation the same?

4 If somebody speaks out of turn do they
a speak before they should?
b say something stupid or offensive?

5 Which of these would be a turn-off to most people?
a garlic
b smelly feet
c bad breath
d dandruff

6 If a building was constructed at the turn of the century, when approximately was it built?
a 1950
b 1890
c 1900

7 If a company has an annual turnover of £25 million does it
a make a profit of £25 million a year?
b do £25 million worth of business a year?

8 What would be a logical way to complete this sentence?

The company took on more staff, which led to greater production, which led to higher profits, which in turn
a meant less money for shareholders.
b meant more money for shareholders.

Listening

You are going to hear four people (two men and two women) talking about talented children. Before you listen to the recording do exercises 1 and 2.

1 Which is the odd one out?

1 gift skill talent present
2 promote encourage identify nurture
3 potentially particularly especially unusually

2 Do you agree or disagree with these statements?

1 ☐ Talented children should be allowed to have a normal childhood.
2 ☐ Children who have excelled often end up as unhappy adults.
3 ☐ It is more often than not the parents who want success for the child, not the child itself.
4 ☐ It is unhealthy for children to be competitive at an early age.
5 ☐ If someone has a special talent, it is their duty to share it with others.

3 🎧 6.2 Listen to the recording once and tick any statements from 2 that at least two people agree with.

4 🎧 6.2 Listen again and put one or two words in each gap.

1 *So if a child is identified as being particularly talented in ...., I don't know, musically or a potentially ...., do you think they should receive .... and training?*

2 *I think the temptation must be great as well if you see your child with a .... skill that obviously they get pleasure from as well, then I think the desire to promote and .... that must be great.*

3 *You could argue that behind every successful child is a ....*

4 *... but now people are on the lookout so much for any .... which they are born with that they are all being snapped up and .... into specific areas.*

Follow up: collocations

5 **a** Look at the tapescript on p.85 and find which nouns collocate with these verbs.

receive	....	get	....
lead	....	achieve	....
waste	....	give	....

b Complete these sentences with an appropriate word or phrase from this list.

a life   education   energy   notoriety   (one's) breath
success   ten years   the joke   the way   welcome

1 The Japanese are leading .... in this particular field.
2 We would like to express our gratitude to our hosts for the warm .... we received from them.
3 He who laughs last has only just got ....
4 They won't listen to you, so don't waste ....
5 They achieved .... through hard work, not luck.
6 Most film stars lead .... of luxury.
7 The man got .... for armed robbery.
8 Don't waste .... Turn off the lights when you leave the room.
9 The woman achieved .... overnight when she admitted her part in the corruption scandal.
10 Mandy had gone to a convent school, where she had received a good ....

7

Language focus

Present perfect SB p.53

1 Correct any mistakes in the verb forms in these conversations.

1 A I always wanted to ask you this, but is that your natural hair colour?

   B I dyed my hair so many times I can't remember what my natural colour is.

2 A I haven't seen you looking so happy since you won that money on the lottery. What happened?

   B A rich aunt I haven't even known I had has sent me some money completely out of the blue.

3 A Did you ever have a sense of déjà-vu?

   B Yes. When I have first met my husband I have had the strangest feeling that I'd met him before. When he walked into the room he has looked very familiar.

4 A I can't believe she's 50.

   B I know. I wonder if she had a face-lift?

5 A Did Cameron decide what he's going to do now he finished university?

   B No, he was awarded a scholarship to do a Master's degree but he decided not to take it up. To my mind he has thrown away a wonderful opportunity.

2 Complete this extract from a magazine article with one of these verbs in the most appropriate form – Past simple or Present perfect simple.

begin	cover	cycle	prove	spend	realize	return (X2)
see	set up	shiver	swelter (=feel very hot)			

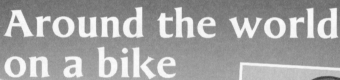

Around the world on a bike

Heinz Stücke ....¹ 37 years traversing the globe on his faithful bicycle, and has no plans to stop now. The 59-year-old ....² to his native Germany just once since 1962, which means he's about to break Marco Polo's record for being away from home for 25 years. He claims he's the most travelled man in the history of the planet.

Stücke got his first taste for the nomadic lifestyle when at the age of eighteen he ....³ 10,000 km around the Mediterranean. He ....⁴ by using pedal power he could travel slowly enough to study each country and its people, and fast enough to cover large distances.

When he ....⁵ home to Hovelhof, his life seemed dull by comparison and he ....⁶

to prepare for a far longer journey – one that ....⁷ to have no end. 'It's the unknown around the corner that turns my wheel,' he says. Stücke ....(now)⁸ every continent except Antarctica and ....⁹ more spectacular sights in his lifetime than most people can reasonably expect to dream of. He ....¹⁰ in the Tropics and ....¹¹ in the Arctic Circle. He has cycled through snow, sand and water.

3 Choose the correct highlighted alternative in these sentences – Present perfect simple or Present perfect continuous.

1 What's that lovely smell? Have you baked / been baking ?

2 A Has anyone seen my pencil sharpener?

   B I haven't touched / been touching it.

   A I never said you had.

3 A I'd like you to meet Eddie.

   B I've heard / been hearing a lot about you.

4 A Have you seen / been seeing Dennis long?

   B Just three months. We met at Sue's flat-warming party.

5 A I hear you went to that new restaurant. What did you think of the food?

   B I've tasted / been tasting worse.

4 Complete these conversations by putting the verbs in brackets in the correct form – Past simple, Present perfect simple, or Present perfect continuous.

1 A You drive very well. How long .... you .... (drive)?

   B I only .... (pass) my test a fortnight ago. Can you drive?

   A I .... (have) lessons. I .... (have) twenty so far. How many .... you .... (have) before you passed?

   B Twenty-five. But I .... (not pass) till my second attempt.

2 A Cigarette, Dave?

   B No, thanks, I .... (give up).

   A Really? When .... you .... (stop)?

   B I .... (not have) a cigarette now for six hours and twenty-two minutes! .... you ever .... (try) to give up?

   A I .... (mean) to stop for ages but I just haven't got enough will power.

🎧 **7.1** Listen, check, and repeat.

Making generalizations SB p.55

5 Read these notes then complete the text by putting one word in each gap.

- Not many young people will have perfect hearing when older
- A small number will be partially deaf
- Most like listening to very loud music
- Not many drive with windows closed
- Stereo usually at maximum
- Police usually do nothing about this

Doctors are worried that very .... ¹ young people will have perfect hearing when they are older, and an unlucky .... ² will be partially deaf. This is because the .... ³ of young people today enjoy listening to loud music, especially when they're on the move.

.... ⁴ anyone seems to drive their car with the windows closed. .... ⁵ speaking, the stereo is at maximum, which causes the car to pulsate with the sound of the bass. As far as many people are concerned, this constitutes noise pollution, but as a .... ⁶, the police are not prepared to do anything about it.

Stücke allows himself few creature comforts, carrying only basic cooking utensils and opting for whatever comes to hand to get some shut-eye. To date he .... ¹² camp in caves, churches, a canoe, and even a phone-box. Also the odd prison cell has been his bed for the night due to suspicious officials on the borders of volatile countries.

Sarah Barnett, Focus magazine

Vocabulary focus

Senses: sight SB p.50

1 a Complete these sentences with *sight* or *view*.

   1 The bride slapped the groom's face in full .... of the wedding guests.

   2 Here are two typical English sayings which have the opposite meaning:
   Absence makes the heart grow fonder;
   Out of .... out of mind.

   3 I am liable to faint at the .... of blood.

   4 When we came over the brow of the hill, the village came into ....

   5 At first .... the problem looked easy.

b Check your answers then complete these sentences with an appropriate phrase from 1a.

   1 Jo had never met anyone like Kevin before. It was love ....

   2 The man was arrested .... of his neighbours.

   3 When we turned the corner, the house ....

   4 Chocolate is not safe in my house unless it's .... If I see it, I eat it.

   5 .... of Carlos putting his arm round his fiancée, Paul flew into a rage.

Senses: sounds SB p.50

Onomatopoeic words are words containing sounds which resemble or suggest what the word refers to, e.g. *whisper, crash*

2 a Try to match the words from this list with the sounds below.

crack   creak   pop   screech   sizzle   thud

   1 a cork coming out of a champagne bottle   ....
   2 sausages frying   ....
   3 a stick breaking underfoot   ....
   4 heavy footsteps on the floor   ....
   5 car tyres when braking suddenly   ....
   6 somebody treading on a loose floorboard   ....

b Complete these sentences with an appropriate word from 2a in an appropriate form.

   1 The snowball flew through the air and landed on the man's back with a soft ....

   2 I could smell eggs frying and hear bacon .... in the frying pan.

   3 There was a loud .... as the footballer, tackled from behind, fell awkwardly on his left leg.

   4 'You'll never hear the end of this!' she .... 'I'll make sure you pay for what you've done!'

   5 The door .... in the wind. It must have blown open.

   6 The children were .... balloons hysterically.

Verb–noun collocations: *express, make,* etc. SB p.55

Here are some more nouns which can collocate with these verbs.

make public / sense
stick to the facts / the rules
put in a claim / a bid (for something)
give priority / (some) thought (to something)
express disagreement / reservations
take somebody's advice / the credit (for something)

3 Complete these sentences with an appropriate noun–verb collocation from the box above in an appropriate form.

   1 In a letter to the chairperson the board of directors .... about relocating the company to a region which had no skilled workforce.

   2 It .... to keep your workforce happy. A happy workforce is more productive.

   3 College lecturers have .... for higher wages arguing that their salaries have fallen way behind those of school teachers.

   4 Don't tell us whose fault you think it was. Just .... Who was operating the machine when the accident happened?

   5 We need to .... to how we are going to promote the product abroad. Any suggestions?

   6 If you ....my............, you'll find another job before you hand in your notice.

Vocabulary expansion

1 a Before you read this magazine article about being a bodyguard, tick (✓) the statements which you think will be mentioned.

Bodyguards need to

1 ☐ take decisions quickly
2 ☐ have 20 / 20 vision
3 ☐ be constantly alert
4 ☐ always be on the lookout for suspicious objects
5 ☐ be tall
6 ☐ be well educated
7 ☐ be trained in first aid
8 ☐ be physically strong

b Now read the article and check your answers.

Idioms with *keep*

1.17 *keep an eye on his hands*

2 Complete the idioms in these sentences with a noun from this list.

ear   an eye   eyes   eyes and ears   face   head   mouth

1 When you are a bodyguard you have to keep your .... open all the time. You need to know exactly what's going on at all times.

2 In critical situations you have to keep your .... You can't afford to panic.

3 If you overhear confidential or private information make sure you keep your .... shut and disclose it to no one.

4 If you keep your .... to the ground, you will always know what's happening and who's saying what. That way you may be able to anticipate trouble.

5 Sometimes you want to laugh out loud at the ridiculous things people say but if you don't keep a straight .... you'll soon be out of a job.

6 When you go into a potentially dangerous situation you must keep your .... peeled for anything even remotely suspicious.

7 If someone asks you to keep .... on a box while they go to the bathroom, it may well contain a bomb.

Looking after the Boss

You've been hired to protect a supermodel from a stalker who's recently issued death threats. At a photoshoot your eyes sweep around the room and come to rest on a
5 particularly shifty-looking character who is concentrating on your client a bit too much. You need to make a split-second decision: do you break through the entourage to
10 immobilize him, or usher the model out of the room? Too late: the attacker's already taken his aim. And the bullet's just hit its target: your client.

15 What went wrong? You got stuck in tunnel vision and failed to keep an eye on his hands, leaving your client vulnerable. In short, you botched up
20 big time.

The best bodyguards are those that call upon all their senses – apart from searching for sudden movement among
25 people, they should also seek out any object and situation that may be threatening. And that could be anything from an egg thrown at a visiting
30 politician or head of state to the ultimate: a bomb or bullet with only one mission – to kill. If, in the above scenario, you had been
35 observant, you would have seen the perpetrator and his gun long before he approached you, enabling offensive, defensive, or avoidance modes.

40 'A properly trained bodyguard will constantly be on the alert, looking for anything that strikes them as suspicious,' says Peter
45 Consterdine, head of Chase Consultants, a company which specializes in training bodyguards. 'If they are with a client in a coffee shop and
50 they spot any potential aggressor making for the establishment they would immediately move their client away.'

55 But if the image of a broken-nosed, tattooed skinhead comes to mind when thinking of a bodyguard, then think again. Today's bodyguards are
60 educated, intelligent, and trained in advanced surveillance techniques, fighting, driving, first aid, and anti-terrorist devices.

Focus magazine

Compound adjectives

1.8 *split-second decision*

3 Complete these sentences with one of these compound adjectives.

dead-end full-scale hard-core high-level low-key
split-second sure-fire

1 I don't want to leave school and get stuck in some .... job. I'm going to go to university and have a career.

2 The wedding was a .... affair. Just a few friends in the registry office.

3 The incident escalated into a .... war.

4 The President of the USA will meet members of the European Commission for .... talks next month.

5 Three hundred .... football supporters, who follow the team wherever they play, will travel to Iceland.

6 I've got a .... solution to the problem. It can't fail.

7 A perfect dive depends on .... timing. It has to be just right.

Listening

You are going to hear three people talking about déjà-vu and premonitions. Before you listen, do exercises 1 and 2.

1 Check that you know the meaning of these words.

> déjà-vu: the feeling that you remember an event or scene that you have not experienced or seen before
>
> premonition: a feeling that something, particularly something unpleasant, is going to happen

2 Answer these questions.

1 Have you ever had déjà-vu?

2 What do you think causes the sensation of déjà-vu?

3 🎧 **7.2** Listen once. How do the speakers answer the questions in 2?

4 🎧 **7.2** Listen again and make more detailed notes about the two explanations.

Follow up: synonyms

> *But if you dreamt it that's very intriguing.*
>
> *That's pretty amazing too.*

5 Replace the word *interesting* with the most suitable word from this list.

amazing engrossing gripping intriguing
mind-boggling

1 There's this really interesting new series on TV. I can't wait for the next episode.

2 The possibilities of genetic engineering are quite interesting.

3 Sorry I'm late. The book I was reading was so interesting that I didn't notice the time.

4 It's an interesting problem and one that I will enjoy solving.

5 I really enjoyed myself on holiday. I had an interesting time.

8

Language focus

what and *it* clauses SB p.61

1 Read this text then complete the sentences below beginning with *what*.

> It is not 100% clear why some parents push their children so hard. Some psychologists believe that they are living out their own frustrated ambitions. They want to realize their own dreams through their children. Parents must remember that their children do not always want success. They should not force their children to do things against their will.

1 *What is not 100% clear is* .... why some parents push their children so hard.

2 .... that they are living out their own frustrated ambitions.

3 .... realize their own dreams through their children.

4 .... that their children do not always want success.

5 .... force their children to do things against their will.

Similar constructions

2 Rewrite these sentences beginning with the word / words in **bold**.

1 The more developed nations produce the most waste.

   It .... produce the most waste.

2 We need to recycle more to cut down on the amount of waste we produce. That's all.

   All .... to recycle.

3 We could all do something to improve the situation; we could reuse our plastic bags.

   Something ....
   to re-use our plastic bags.

4 It will only work if everyone does their bit.

   The only way ....
   if everyone does their bit.

5 The amount of packaging that manufacturers use really annoys me.

   It .... really annoys me.

The future SB p.63

3 Choose the two correct possible alternatives from the three highlighted.

1 The government will need to / will be needing to / are going to need to pay more attention to public opinion if they are to be re-elected.

2 We discuss / are going to discuss / will be discussing the proposed changes in two months' time.

3 A How are you travelling?

   B I will travel / am going to travel / am travelling first class as the company will pay / is paying / will be paying.

4 I expect we will be seeing / are seeing / will see more of you now that you've moved to the area.

5 It has been announced that 100 jobs are going to be lost / are being lost / will be lost in the coming year.

4 Put the verbs in brackets in the most appropriate form.

1 Slow down Ethan. You .... (finish) before the rest of us have even started.

2 Thousands of pounds worth of damage .... (do) if the rain continues.

3 You look absolutely shattered. Why don't you take the weight off your feet and I .... (make) us a nice cup of tea?

4 Holly and Tim have finally named the day. They .... (get married) in June.

5 What day .... your birthday .... (fall) on next year?

6 I won't be able to give you a lift tomorrow. My car .... (service).

5 Correct any mistakes in the verb forms in these sentences.

1 What will our lives be like in the future?

2 In 2025 most people probably will have worked at home.

3 The quality of television will have improved so much that most cinemas will end up closing.

4 In 30 years' time the standard of public transport will improve. As a result the rush hour will be being reduced to a distant memory.

5 A vaccine for AIDS will probably have been discovered.

6 In 50 years' time people will still have got married, although divorce rates will continue to rise.

7 By 2025, although children will be being freed from the classroom by new technology, teachers will still continue to play an important role in education.

8 Fewer people are going to study arts subjects at university. People will be encouraged to take practical subjects such as sciences, economics, and engineering.

🎧 **8.1** Listen, check, and repeat.

6 Complete this text with a verb from this list in an appropriate future form.

be ~~become~~ breathe demand eat encourage (=cause) increase reduce replant use

WHAT DO THE EXPERTS PREDICT LIFE WILL BE LIKE IN 20 YEARS' TIME?

FOOD

Vegetable proteins like Quark *will have become* [1] an established alternative to meat and animal products. Only 10 per cent of the population will be totally vegetarian but the rest of us .... [2] very little meat.

Awareness of the dangers of pesticides, artificial fertilizers, intensive farming, and food processing .... [3], and we .... [4] organically-grown, chemical-free fruit and vegetables. Pure unadulterated food will be the ultimate luxury. There will be a greater emphasis on eating for health, and diet .... [5] both to keep fit and counter disease. Dieting to achieve a fashionable figure will be a thing of the past. Looking healthy – not thin – .... [6] what matters.

THE ENVIRONMENT

Unless we find a way of stopping global warming, the world will be a hotter – and possibly smaller – place to live. Scientists predict that the temperature of the earth as a whole will be around two degrees higher. This .... [7] the polar ice-caps to melt and could put much of Europe in danger from flooding. At least around 500,000 species around the world will have become extinct. But pollution from cars, industry and power .... [8] to a minimum, so we .... [9] cleaner air. Rivers should be fresh enough for fish to thrive in and the sea will be less polluted. Recycled goods will be common and aerosols and ozone-destroying chemicals a thing of the past. Rainforests .... [10] (regularly) and subsidies offered to poorer countries willing to conserve their wildlife and develop environmentally sound industries and farming methods.

Woman

Vocabulary focus

Crime SB p.60

1 a Do you think these sentences are True or False?

1 ☐ In order to fire a gun, you have to pull the trigger.
2 ☐ If you lead somebody astray, you encourage them to do bad things.
3 ☐ If you are a hardened criminal, it means you are doing or have done hard labour, like, for example, breaking up rocks.
4 ☐ If you turn to crime you begin a way of life that involves crime.
5 ☐ If you commit a petty crime, you will go to prison for a long time.
6 ☐ If a judge lets somebody off he or she sends the person to prison.
7 ☐ If someone has to serve a life sentence they will have to stay in prison for the rest of their lives.

b Complete this text with a word or phrase from 1a in an appropriate form.

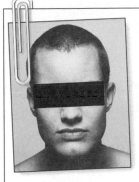

Robert Millar committed his first criminal offence when he was only eight years old. Like many other young people who end up in the prison system he .... 1 through boredom. He said he had done it because there was nothing to do on the housing estate where he lived and that it had just been 'a bit of fun'. This first offence was not, as one might imagine, a .... 2 crime, like stealing sweets from the corner shop. It was a serious offence. He had stolen a car and raced around the estate endangering people's lives.

Because of his age, Millar could not be prosecuted in Britain. Also it was thought that he might have been .... 3 by other older boys on the estate. So he was .... 4 with a caution.

However, twenty years later and Millar had become a .... 5 criminal, never out of gaol for more than a few weeks. He is presently serving a life sentence for the murder of an unarmed police officer, who was working undercover. In his defence Millar had argued that he hadn't known the dead man was a police officer, and that he had .... 6 in self-defence.

Vocabulary expansion

1 a You are going to read an article about the United States and guns. Before you read it match these numbers with the information you think they go with.

1 ☐	young people aged 15–24 killed with a firearm in 1996	a	68
2 ☐	guns owned by students	b	5,500
3 ☐	privately held guns	c	14,000
4 ☐	homicides committed with firearms in 1996	d	1,000,000
5 ☐	children under 4 killed with a firearm in 1996	e	200,000,000

b As you read the text, check your ideas.

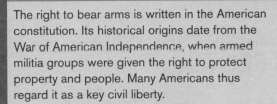

America and the gun

The right to bear arms is written in the American constitution. Its historical origins date from the War of American Independence, when armed militia groups were given the right to protect property and people. Many Americans thus regard it as a key civil liberty.   5

Anti-gun groups, however, argue that this right is now out-dated and should be revoked. They present the following alarming facts to support their argument: 10

• There are an estimated 200 million privately held guns in the USA. Of these one million are in the hands of students — every day guns are taken into high schools, sometimes with fatal consequences.

• In 1996 14,000 homicides were committed with   15
firearms. Of those killed, 68 were children under the age of four and over 5,500 were between 15 and 24 years old.

• The highest death rate per capita is for men aged between 20 and 24. This runs at 30 per   20
100,000.

• The most likely people to be shot are black males who come from low-income, inner-city areas.

It does seem that public opinion in the United States is changing against the liberal gun laws,   25
with many newspapers now questioning the wisdom of continuing to permit such widespread gun ownership. But any change, if and when it does come, will not come overnight.

Prefixes: anti-

1.7 anti-gun groups

> The prefix anti- can have different meanings:
> 1 opposed to / against; preventing: anti-nuclear; anti-drug
> 2 the opposite of: antihero

2 a Complete these sentences with an appropriate word from this list.

anticlimax anticlockwise antiperspirants antiseptic
anti-social

1 ☐ To open the door, insert the key in the lock and turn it in an .... direction.
2 ☐ .... don't completely stop sweating but they do help to control it.
3 ☐ Christmas is always a bit of an .... after all the build up, isn't it?
4 ☐ Juvenile delinquents will often display .... behaviour from an early age.
5 ☐ If you cut yourself, you should clean the wound , then dab .... on it to prevent infection.

b Decide if the anti- words have meaning 1 or 2. Write your answer in each box.

Latin phrases

1.19 per capita

3 a The following Latin phrases are in common use in English. Match them with their meanings.

1 ☐ ad nauseam   a for each year
2 ☐ per annum   b for each person
3 ☐ per capita   c medical examination to determine cause of death
4 ☐ post-mortem   d again and again so that it becomes irritating
5 ☐ status quo   e in the opposite way to what has just been said
6 ☐ vice versa   f state of affairs as it is now

b Check your answers then complete these sentences with an appropriate phrase from 3a.

1 The .... examination revealed that the man had died of a heart attack.
2 Megan and Ted talked about their holiday .... and bored everyone to death.
3 Interest will be paid at a rate of 5.5% ....
4 The arrangement should work to both our advantage: I help you out when you need it and ....
5 Average .... income is likely to stabilize during the next quarter.

Listening

You are going to hear two recordings in which Anthony and Carole (who are in their 50s) and Lisa (who is 18) talk about parental control.

1 Before you listen, answer these questions.

1 Do you think parents should lay down rules and regulations for their children to follow?
2 Were there lots of rules and regulations in your house when you were growing up?
3 Do you / Would you bring up your own children differently in this respect?

2 🎧 **8.2** Listen to the recordings once. How do the speakers answer the questions in 1?

3 🎧 **8.2** Listen again and put between one and four words in each gap.

1 Carole thinks that if children don't have rules and regulations they feel .... and
....
2 Carole thinks that her parents imposed so many rules because they didn't ....
3 Anthony's children .... than he had.
4 Lisa thinks children need to learn rules ....
5 Although Lisa didn't like all the rules and regulations that her parents imposed she realized that they were for ....

Follow up: /t/ and /d/ at word boundaries

> In natural speech when a word ends in /t/ or /d/ and is followed by another word, the /t/ or /d/ is not usually pronounced in the following circumstances:
> 1 when the next word begins with /p/, /b/, /t/, /d/, /k/, /g/, for example: hard time
> 2 when the /t/ or /d/ occurs between two other consonants. For example: must be; old gun

4 a Look at these extracts from the recordings and cross out any /t/ and /d/ sounds you think will not be pronounced.

1 Not being a parent myself …
2 … if they don't have those boundaries they just seem to go a bit crazy …
3 I didn't feel secure …
4 … things I knew I should and shouldn't do …
5 … seemed to be based on my parents not trusting me to behave …
6 … because they assumed I would do something when in fact it never crossed my mind to do that …

b 🎧 **8.3** Listen and check your answers.

9

Language focus

Adverbs of degree SB p.67

1 In these sentences the adverbs of degree have been left out. Choose the most appropriate adverb from the alternatives given in brackets. Then write the adverb in the correct place in the sentence.

1 It was a warm summer but the day Marta got married
particularly
was/hot. (absolutely / particularly)

2 This piece of work is unsatisfactory. You'll have to do it again. (quite / fairly)

3 You're wrong. I didn't tell Mark. Zoe did. (very / completely)

4 She felt tired when she'd finished doing the pile of ironing so she decided to have a rest. (too / rather)

5 I'd love to have a sports car but they're expensive to run. (absolutely / extremely)

6 She had recovered from the flu when she went down with a cold. (quite / hardly)

7 One of the questions on the exam paper was difficult to answer. (totally / too)

8 I have enough money for myself. I can't lend you any. (scarcely / slightly)

🎧 **9.1** Listen, check, and repeat.

2 Correct any mistakes in word order in these sentences.

1 I wanted to go very much to the concert.

2 That was a review rather interesting.

3 He sings in such a way that it's quite impossible to hear all the words.

4 The group hardly had started playing when the lights went out.

5 The concert was perfect absolutely. I couldn't fault it.

6 I really hoped the band would play an encore.

7 I know nobody else does but I like rather his music.

8 Although it is a quite good song, I doubt it'll get into the charts.

Formal and informal style SB p.69

3 Rewrite the underlined words and phrases in a more informal style.

1 A (on the phone) Hello. Is that Mrs Allen?
 B <u>To whom am I speaking</u>?

 ....

2 Mel and I talked about our holidays, boyfriends, and other <u>related subjects</u>.

 ....

3 <u>Not realizing</u> who he was, I didn't speak to him.

 ....

4 <u>I would be extremely pleased</u> to play tennis with you tomorrow.

 ....

5 <u>In my view</u> the traffic situation has <u>deteriorated</u> because <u>more and more roads are being constructed</u>.

 ....

4 Rewrite the underlined words and phrases in these sentences in a more formal style using appropriate words from this list. Sometimes you will need to change the word order.

announce   apologize   disembark   ensure   the event
have   the marriage   personal belongings   provided

1 (Notice) Before you <u>get off the plane</u> please <u>make sure</u> that you<u>'ve got</u> all your <u>stuff</u> with you.

 ....

2 (Wedding invitation) Mr and Mrs Black are pleased to <u>tell you that</u> their daughter Elizabeth <u>is getting married</u> to James Bishop on Friday 16th June.

 ....

3 (Letter) Dear Sirs,
 <u>We're very sorry that we haven't answered</u> your letter sooner.

 ....

4 (Notice) <u>If there's a</u> fire, do not use the lift.

 ....

5 (Notice) Put your litter in the bins <u>we've given you to use</u>.

 ....

5 Read this review of a CD by the Irish group the Corrs.

CD Review: *The Corrs*

Quite how the Corrs managed to find themselves in the frame as one of the world's biggest bands is a mystery. There must be an awful lot of folk out there who like safe, wishy-washy pop songs trotted out by a squeaky-clean production line that thinks living dangerously is building a house on the site of a drained marsh.

Anyway, moving swiftly on. Before the rapid dissection of *In Blue* – the follow-up to *Talk on Corners* begins, let's hear it from the horses' mouths.

'Every band says their latest record is the best, but I really believe it,' says Andrea. 'It's who we are and we're really proud of it. It reflects how we've progressed and what we've learned.'

Over to Jim: 'I suppose there are a lot of different vibes. I think a few people are going to be surprised by that.' Excuse me? Time for a reality check. The first rule of Corrs law is always to expect the expected.

Watered-down

With the exception of the radio-friendly *Radio*, all the up-tempo numbers are sugary, lost-love, found-love tales. But enough of this cruelty, when the Corrs decide to slow things down a bit, they have got a couple of decent songs. *One Night* could have almost been written by The Carpenters.

Anyway, they've managed to earn a few quid by playing it straight so far, so good luck to them. One question, though. If all these millions of people have bought a Corrs record, how come I've never met anyone who admits to actually owning one?

BBC News Online

6 Match these more formal equivalents with the informal highlighted words and phrases in the text.

1 I find that very hard to believe ....

2 from those who are directly involved ....

3 one or two good ....

4 produced without much thought ....

5 a considerable amount of money ....

6 to change the subject ....

7 reduce the tempo ....

8 I wish them every success ....

9 a little ....

10 many people in the world ....

Vocabulary focus

Adjectives with similar forms SB p.72

1 Complete these sentences with an appropriate word from the list below.

classic classical comic comical economic economical

1 It is more .... to buy the bigger bottle.

2 A Who is your favourite .... composer?
  B I'd find it hard to choose between Mozart and Beethoven.

3 Charlie Chaplin was a great .... actor as well as being a great director. He looked quite .... in his ill-fitting clothes.

4 I prefer a .... novel to anything modern. Dickens, Tolstoy, and de Maupassant are among my favourites.

5 It is not advisable to take financial risks in the current .... climate.

2 a Here are some words with similar forms. Read these definitions.

complement:	go together; combine well with
compliment:	praise
dependant:	somebody who relies on somebody else for a home, money, food, etc
dependent:	needing the support of something in order to continue operating
disinterested:	impartial
uninterested:	not interested, bored
dissatisfied:	not pleased with
unsatisfied:	disappointed because you have not got what you hoped for
disused:	no longer used
misused:	incorrectly used

b Choose the correct highlighted alternative in these sentences.

1 Applicants for the post must be unmarried males without dependants / dependents .

2 Sheila was dissatisfied / unsatisfied with the reply she got from the travel agency to her letter of complaint. She had expected an apology at the very least.

3 I'm giving you totally uninterested / disinterested advice. I have nothing to gain whatever you decide.

4 The word 'less' is commonly disused / misused nowadays. The grammatically correct form before plural countable nouns is 'fewer', not 'less'.

5 She is a very shy person whereas he is an extrovert. They make a good couple as they compliment / complement each other well.

6 I was totally uninterested / disinterested in the topic of the programme and switched channels after a few minutes.

7 Most of us feel unsatisfied / dissatisfied with the way we look , but not everyone goes on to do something about it.

8 I'd like to compliment / complement you on your speech. It was excellent.

9 The expression 'It's raining cats and dogs' has fallen into disuse / misuse . No one says it any more.

10 The charity is totally dependant / dependent on public funding.

Vocabulary expansion

1 Read this review, ignoring the blanks for the moment.
   How many stars do you think the music critic gave it?

   ☆   ☆☆☆   ☆☆☆☆☆

2 Complete the review with a word or phrase from this list.

   catchy   in the charts   lyrical   pop music   review   tracks

CD Review: *The Beatles – 1*

The Beatles in 1964

More than 30 years after The Beatles split up, the popularity
of the Fab Four is undiminished.

In the pop pantheon the Beatles are gods, and a true

5 .... [1] of this compilation album is impossible
because the band and their music seem beyond criticism.

The Beatles' music does not simply have a timeless quality – it is
hard to imagine a time when their music did not exist.

It is worth listening to the .... [2] in

10 chronological order and pretending the album is on an
old-fashioned LP because the change in the music and the
.... [3] content is quite startling.

BBC News Online

The Beatles in 1967

The early songs are lyrically naïve but that simplicity has given
The Beatles a universality no other band has managed to achieve.

15 From a recording point of view, the simple four-track, sometimes
mono, sound and structure of the early songs seem dated, but the
musical quality is undeniable.

In the 1960s The Beatles were re-writing the rules of popular
music as they went along, breaking new barriers with each and
every release.

20

By the time *Ticket to Ride* arrives on the album, equating to less
then two years after their first single release, John, Paul, George,
and Ringo had re-defined .... [4].

The album is filled with creativity, and climaxes with

25 *All You Need Is Love*, perhaps the perfect pop record –
.... [5], playful, joyous, and irreverent.

It still sounds utterly contemporary and only accentuates the
dearth of good bands and songs .... [6] today.

The 27 tracks on the album completely fill the CD and while

30 that equates to around 70 minutes of music in total it is enough
to last anyone a lifetime.

Word-building

3 a The following nouns appeared in the review.
     Complete the table with the missing verbs
     and adjectives.

NOUN	VERB	ADJECTIVE
compilation		X
criticism		
simplicity		
universality	X	
creativity		

b What are the nouns from these verbs?

   1 clarify   ....
   2 rely   ....
   3 be unable   ....
   4 imitate   ....
   5 repeat   ....

c Complete these sentences with an appropriate word from 3a or 3b.

1 The best pop songs are .... and catchy.

2 The song has three verses and a chorus which is .... after each verse.

3 His songs are just cheap .... of Beatles' tunes.

4 Good songwriters, like poets, are ....

5 The review of her latest album was highly ....

Adjectives with the prefix *un-*

> **1.2** *undiminished*

4 a Do you think these sentences are True or False?

1 ☐ If something is unfathomable it is too simple.

2 ☐ If somebody's popularity is undiminished they are still as popular as they used to be.

3 ☐ If a journey is uneventful it is unpleasant.

4 ☐ If somebody says something uncharitable to you it will hurt you.

5 ☐ If somebody is described as unassuming they are not very knowledgeable.

6 ☐ If you wear something unflattering it doesn't suit you.

7 ☐ If a person is unattainable they are shy and introverted.

8 ☐ If a novel is uninspired it says nothing new.

b Check your answers then complete these sentences with an adjective from 4a.

1 Before The Beatles achieved fame their lives were quite .... and ordinary.

2 Few pop stars strike me as being modest, ... sort of people.

3 In my opinion the shorter hairstyles The Beatles sported in the early 60s made them more attractive than their hippy image, which was quite ....

4 Many young girls dream of going out with their favourite pop stars even though they are quite ....

5 The group's last album was totally .... and really not worth buying.

6 Why 90s groups like the Spice Girls became so popular is an .... mystery to many music critics.

7 Despite the fact that the group are all in their sixties, they still manage to perform with .... vigour.

8 The review was full of negative, ... remarks about the group's lack of musical talent.

Listening

You are going to hear someone talking about music.

1 🎧 **9.2** Listen to the recording once and decide which statement is the best summary of the speaker's views.

a The best way to listen to music is on a Walkman.

b Music can fulfil many different purposes.

c Music can help you get over depression.

▶ **Note** Bloomingdale's is a large American department store.

2 🎧 **9.2** Listen again and decide whether these statements are True or False according to the speaker.

1 ☐ Music can change your mood.

2 ☐ The first time he listened to music on his Walkman he was disappointed.

3 ☐ The music reaches its climax as he gets to the top of the escalator.

4 ☐ Drinking is a better way of getting over depression than listening to music.

5 ☐ Music always cheers him up.

Follow up: metaphorical language

3 Look at these examples of metaphorical language from the recording and choose the best meanings.

1 *Music is a* drug . *It's mood-altering.*

a something that is addictive

b something that makes you better

c something that changes how you feel

2 *It's like* supplying an orchestral score to your life .

a It makes your life seem more dramatic

b It gives you a reason for living

c It makes you feel happier

3 *Just as the music is* swelling ...

a just becoming audible

b reaching a crescendo

c getting quieter

4 *I can* pump myself up *during a workout.*

a make the adrenaline flow

b lift heavy weights

c fill one's lungs with oxygen

10

Language focus

as and *like* SB p.75

1 Complete the sentences with *like*, *as*, or *as if*.

1 You can still live .... a king in some parts of the world on a small amount of money.

2 Samantha has been working .... a travel rep for a large international company for some years now.

3 He spoke to me .... I would understand every word he said although it was obvious that I was a foreigner.

4 .... most people who come from northern Europe, I was desperate to feel the sun on my body after a long, cold winter.

5 You can feel .... a foreigner in your own town in summer .... there are so many tourists around.

6 A What's that?

   B It's actually sun cream but I use it .... a mosquito repellent.

Story-telling: Historic present SB p.77

2 Complete this extract from a novel with a verb from this list in the most appropriate form – Present simple or Present continuous.

---

adjust   count out   drip   get up   happen   lay (X2)
leave   look at   play up (= not function properly)
pull away   say   walk

I pull into the parking lot in front of the flower shop. There is a light breeze blowing. Inside the store a man is bending down, carefully checking the leaves of a small green plant. He .... [1] slowly and painfully as I enter.

'Evening,' he .... [2]. 'Help you?'

'I'd like some of those roses. Give me a dozen. No, better make it two dozen.'

'Two dozen roses, yessir.' He is heavy-set and bald, maybe in his early sixties. He .... [3] stiffly, hardly bending his knees. The joints of his fingers are swollen with arthritis.

'The air-conditioning .... [4],' he says. As he passes by the control unit on the wall, he .... [5] a switch but nothing .... [6]. He begins lifting roses carefully from a bucket, and when he has counted twenty-four, he .... [7] them on a sheet of plastic on the counter.

'Gift wrap 'em for ya?'

'No. Plastic is fine.'

He .... [8] me for a moment. 'Do I know you from someplace? I'm sure I know you from someplace.'

'I don't think so.'

'You from around here? Canaan, maybe? Monterey?'

'No. Someplace else.' I am about to use my credit card but decide not to. Instead, I .... [9] the cash and .... [10] it on the counter.

'Someplace else,' he says, nodding as if it has some deep, inner meaning for him. 'Must be a big place. I meet a lot of fellers from there.'

But I .... (already) [11] the store. As I .... [12] I can see him at the window, staring after me. Behind me, water .... [13] gently from the rose stems onto the floor.

Every Dead Thing, John Connolly

Performative verbs Language Commentary p.79

3 Choose the correct highlighted alternative.

1 The travel company apologized to put / for putting the price of the holiday up at the last minute.

2 The bedroom is quite unsuitable. I demand to see / seeing the manager.

3 I insisted to have / on having a room with a view.

4 If you are not satisfied with your accommodation, I advise you speak / you to speak to your travel representative.

5 If you want a good value holiday, we recommend you go / on going to Cuba.

6 The letter congratulated me on winning / in winning the competition – a two-week cruise in the Caribbean.

7 Jasmine thanked me profusely for taking / on taking her to the airport.

8 The passenger objected to have / to having to sit in the smoking section of the aeroplane.

9 The passenger refused sitting down / to sit down when the flight attendant asked him to.

10 Emily hotly denied using / to use the last of my sun-tan lotion when I accused her.

11 I suggest to have / having a rest before we start sightseeing in earnest.

12 Visitors to the cathedral are forbidden of taking / to take flash photographs.

4 Rewrite these sentences using a performative verb from 3.

1 You are not to see him again. Is that understood?

I .... him again.

2 I'm very sorry I didn't tell you sooner.

I .... sooner.

3 Well done! You passed your test.

I'd like to .... your test.

4 It was really nice of you to come.

....

5 I want to speak to whoever is in charge this minute.

I .... to whoever is in charge.

6 I think we should go home now before the traffic builds up.

I .... home now before the traffic builds up.

7 Medical experts say people should stay indoors during the hottest part of the day.

Medical experts .... indoors during the hottest part of the day.

🎧 **10.1** Listen, check, and repeat.

Vocabulary focus

Compound nouns SB p.78

1 Complete the crossword using these clues.

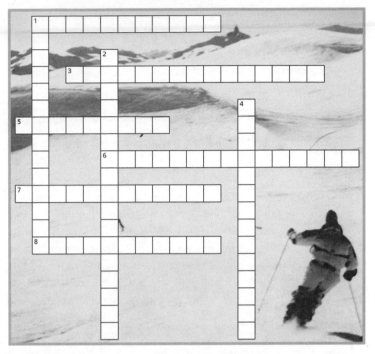

Across

1 When I was a child I used to save up the ...... I got from my parents every Saturday for my summer holidays.

3 and 6 The flight attendant asked passengers to turn off their ...... and ...... as their use could interfere with the aircraft controls.

5 Before the plane took off we had to put our seats in an upright position and fasten our ....

7 If you want an activity holiday in January and are into skiing, snowboarding, and other ......, Colorado is the place to go.

8 Young people can find clean affordable accommodation in a ....

Down

1 Graham would have liked to have gone on an exotic adventure holiday but it was beyond his means. An all-inclusive ...... would have to do.

2 Don't carry cash with you when you go on holiday. ...... are a much safer alternative.

4 Have you packed your ......, Matthew? They say the sea will be just the right temperature for a dip.

Vocabulary expansion

1 Read this extract from a short story and answer these questions.

   1 Why has the writer gone to Palenque?

   2 Why does no one visit Palenque in mid-August?

   3 Which adjectives, a, b, or c, best describe Palenque?

   a remote and wild

   b oppressive and dangerous

   c awe-inspiring and verdant

Worst Journeys

NOBODY GOES TO PALENQUE IN MID-AUGUST, and what we were doing there then remains a mystery to me. Perhaps it was just a case of bad planning. But there we were, and we experienced it in its full force. The minute we
5 stepped outside in the morning the heat struck us, bowled us over like a blast furnace. Our jeans, which we'd washed out the night before, were stiff as boards, dry as clay in the morning sun. But my hair never felt dry the entire time I was in Palenque: it was always soaked with sweat. As we
10 walked to the ruins, the people swung in their hammocks, expressionless, barely moving, dead-looking, brains boiled. The jungle of Palenque was not like that of the highlands. Here there were no hills, no vistas, no gentle rolling of the land. In Palenque you were at the bottom of a pit of the
15 lowlands, enclosed in a jungle prison. No breeze blew through this hollow. It felt ominous, treacherous, omnivorous, and indifferent, as if it would swallow you with a single gulp. If you stood still for just a moment, vines would engulf you, snakes would poison you, small
20 crawling things would devour you, the air would be stolen from you. And you would be forgotten.

Mary Morris

Similes

> **1.7** *stiff as boards* **1.7** *dry as clay*

> A simile is a comparison of one thing with another using *like* or *as*. For example: *He lives like a king; She's as cold as ice.*

2 a Complete these common similes with a word from this list.

ditchwater	gold	the hills	nails	pie	Punch	a sheet

   1 as good as ....   5 as white as ....

   2 as hard as ....   6 as easy as ....

   3 as dull as ....   7 as old as ....

   4 as pleased as ....

b Check your answers then complete these sentences with an appropriate simile from 2a.

   1 That joke's .... I've heard it a million times.

   2 A Did the letter contain bad news?

     B It must have. Jane went .... when she read it.

   3 A Did the children misbehave?

     B No, they were ....

   4 Criticism never affects Joanne. She's ....

   5 A I'll never get the hang of this!

     B Don't be ridiculous. It's ....

Adjectives ending in *-ous*

> **1.16** *ominous* **1.16** *treacherous*
>
> **1.17** *omnivorous*

3 a Do you think these statements are True or False?

   1 If you have an omnivorous diet, you will eat all kinds of food.

   2 If you behave in an impetuous way, you think carefully before you do something.

   3 If someone says they have an announcement to make and this is followed by an ominous silence, people are expecting to hear bad news.

   4 If a film critic described a film as tedious, people would rush to see it.

   5 If somebody is described as treacherous, they would not make a good friend.

b Check your answers then complete these sentences with an appropriate adjective from 3a.

   1 Look at those black clouds! They look ....

   2 Don't swim there. The currents are .... Someone drowned there only last month.

   3 She's an .... reader. She'll read anything and everything.

   4 I thought the speech was never going to end. It was so ....

   5 Don't you think you're being a bit ....? You've only known each other a few weeks and already you're talking about marriage.

Listening

You are going to hear Sean talking about his trip to the Inca site of Machu Picchu in Peru.

1 🎧 **10.2** Listen to the recording once and decide which of these statements best summarizes his feelings about the trip.

a It was worth all the effort.
b On the whole, it was a disappointment.
c The whole experience was wonderful.

2 Match the highlighted words from the recording with their meanings.

1 ... *the ancient sacred* site ...
2 ... *it was* high season *at the time*
3 ... *this deserted mountain* pass
4 ... *thousands of people pushing and* shoving ...
5 ... *all with their* rucksacks *and their cameras*
6 ... *people were* elbowing *other people out of the way* ...
7 ... *experience and* appreciate *this properly* ...

a ☐ a road or way over or through mountains
b ☐ bag carried on the back by walkers and climbers
c ☐ enjoy the good qualities of something
d ☐ push roughly with the elbows
e ☐ the time of year when most people visit a place
f ☐ pushing roughly
g ☐ place where a building or town is situated

3 🎧 **10.2** Listen again and answer these questions.

1 How had Sean arrived at the site?
2 Where was the best view of the sunrise from?
3 Why were there so many other people there?
4 What was everyone's main objective?
5 What was the atmosphere like at 'The Sun Gate'? Why?
6 Why did he move to another place?
7 Was he glad that he did? Why / Why not?

Follow up: verb pairs

... thousands of people pushing and shoving

4 Some verbs are often used together with another verb which has a similar or related meaning. Try to match the verbs 1–7 with the verbs in a–g.

1 ☐ shouting and   a groaning
2 ☐ cursing and   b choosing
3 ☐ moaning and   c puffing
4 ☐ picking and   d ahhing
5 ☐ huffing and   e yelling
6 ☐ umming and   f dining
7 ☐ wining and   g swearing

5 Check your answers, then complete these sentences with an appropriate combination in an appropriate form.

1 Peter .... Rachel every night for a month before asking her to marry him.

2 The neighbours were obviously having a huge row judging by all the .... that was going on.

3 You have to take any job you can get these days. You can't .... like you used to be able to.

4 After a lot of .... Mick reluctantly agreed to help with the preparations for the party.

5 Joe was .... under his breath. He was obviously having trouble putting up the shelf.

6 When I got to the top of the hill I was .... I hadn't realized how unfit I was till that moment.

11

Language focus

Modals: *must, can, can't + have* SB p.81

1 Complete these mini-dialogues with the most appropriate modal – *must, can, can't + have* – and the correct form of the verb in brackets.

1 A I can't remember where I've put my passport.

   B It must be somewhere. You .... (lose) it. You'll just have mislaid it.

2 A (Opening the fridge) Oh good, there's some milk. I thought you said there wasn't any.

   B Roy .... (buy) some when he was out.

3 A Who has left all this dirty washing-up in the sink?

   B It .... (be) Gabi.

   A No, it .... (be) Gabi because she's been at her parents' all weekend.

   B Then it .... only .... (be) Alice because it certainly wasn't me!

4 A Tony told me he was emigrating to Australia.

   B He .... (be) serious. He hates hot weather. He .... (pull) your leg.

5 A Jeff said he'd be here at three and it's half past. Where on earth .... he .... (get) to?

   B He .... hardly .... (forget). He knows how important it is.

🎧 **11.1** Listen, check, and repeat.

Relative clauses SB p.83

2 The sentences below can end in two different ways. Choose the best endings from this list and write them in the spaces provided. Add an appropriate relative pronoun where necessary.

---
has the best weather   said he wouldn't be able to come
you'd buy if you could afford it   Pete recommended we go to
most tourists come   she is going on holiday with
~~won the award for best design~~   we celebrated your birthday

---

1 Which is the car

   a *which/that won the award for best design* ....?

   b ....?

2 What's the name of that restaurant

   a ....?

   b ....?

3 Which is the season

   a ....?

   b ....?

4 Is it David or Alan

   a ....?

   b ....?

3 Correct any mistakes in the relative clauses in this text. You will sometimes need to add or cross out commas.

> I remember when I was young, we always went on holiday to
>   *which*
> Kingscliff, <u>that</u> is a small seaside town north of Sydney. We
> always went in September when it was quieter. We used to stay in
> a holiday cabin, which was right on the beach. There were five or
> six cabins in the complex we stayed. Ours had two bedrooms one
> of whose had a sea view.
>
> On the first Saturday in September, we'd drive there in our old
> Ford, which always broke down on the way. My sister Anne whom
> was always car-sick used to sit in the front. Our dog that was
> a German Shepherd called Honey sat in the back between Mum
> and me. I remember we always stopped at a place, that we could
> have a barbecue, to break the journey. I enjoyed those beach
> holidays when I was a child.

Articles SB p.85

4 You are going to read a newspaper article. Follow these instructions for each section of the text.

a Choose the correct highlighted alternative.

Swedes find it pays to put up with ads on the phone.

SO THERE YOU ARE, whispering sweet nothings down a / the [1] line to your loved one, when in butts a / the [2] stranger. A crossed line? An / The [3] operator who has made a mistake? No, a commercial break for bacon crisps.

In Sweden, it seems, listening to advertisements is a / the [4] small price to pay for an otherwise free phone-call. And an / the [5] idea could be coming soon to a / the [6] line near you.

b Cross out any articles which should not be there.

It's going to be huge,' said Peter Broden of Gratistelefon, a [1] Stockholm company that recently became the world's first to offer the [2] free calls to anyone willing to put up with adverts.

'The [3] people aren't irritated by it at all. The [4] young like it because they like the phone anyway, and this is free. The [5] old like it because now they can call their long-lost friends at the [6] other end of the country. And advertisers love it – they get a [7] captive audience,' he said.

c Add an appropriate article where necessary.

How does it work? Callers dial ... [1] toll-free access number and give the computer the number they want. ... [2] 10-second advert plays while they are connected, another after ... [3] minute, and a new one every three minutes thereafter.

Advertisers include ... [4] snack manufacturer, ... [5] cinema chain and ... [6] children's charity. Between ... [7] 10 and 15 telecommunications companies around Europe have expressed ... [8] keen interest in applying the idea, Mr Broden said. 'I'm afraid this is one you definitely haven't heard ... [9] last of.'

John Henley, The Guardian

Vocabulary focus

Memory and memories SB p.82

1 Try to choose the correct highlighted alternative in these sentences.

1 I hadn't heard the song for such a long time. It really took me away / back .

2 When they were at school they had to learn poems by heart / memory .

3 The documentary was a harsh reminiscence / reminder of the horrors of war.

4 It's nice to get together like this. It brings back reminders / memories of when we all went on holiday to Ibiza.

5 A Have you seen this person before?
B His face looks familiar / memorable but the name doesn't sound a horn / ring a bell .

6 She racked her head / brain to try to remember where she had seen the man before.

7 Julie's phone number? Yes, just a minute. It's on the end / tip of my tongue. I'll remember it in a minute.

8 As soon as Josh looked at the exam paper, his mind went blank / vacant .

9 I've got a memory like a hole in the head / a sieve . When somebody tells me something it goes in my / one ear and out my / the other. I have to write things down to jog / jostle my memory.

10 On one lasting / memorable occasion Charlie told his boss exactly what he thought of him.

Words often confused SB p.84

2 a Check that you know the difference in meaning between the pairs of words in this list.

argue / discuss	present / actual
date / appointment	remember / remind
kind / sympathetic	souvenir / memory
on the contrary / on the other hand	

b Choose the correct highlighted alternative in these sentences.

1 Did he really say that? What were his present / actual words?

2 Mathew and Sally have been arguing / discussing all evening about the score of a football match that happened 10 years ago!

3 Will you remember / remind me to Patrick when you see him?

4 We have many happy souvenirs / memories of our years in Africa.

5 The police were sympathetic / kind to my complaint about the noise but said that they could do nothing about it.

6 A Jayne won't be able to come tomorrow. She's got a(n) date / appointment with Robbie.

   B I didn't know they were going out together.

7 Flying is expensive. On the contrary / On the other hand it's much faster than any other method of transport.

8 The actual / present Prime Minister has been in power for two years.

9 When you've finished discussing / arguing the pros and cons of Chinese and Italian food – maybe we could have something to eat?

10 She remembers / reminds me of you when you were that age.

11 She's such a sympathetic / kind person. She always has time for other people.

12 Jackie's house is full of cheap, tacky souvenirs / memories from all the places she's ever been to.

13 I don't think travelling by train is tiresome. On the contrary / On the other hand, you often meet interesting people on trains.

14 Tomorrow afternoon won't be possible. I've got a(n) appointment / date with my bank manager. I need to ask for an overdraft.

Vocabulary expansion

1 Read this newspaper article about memory and decide on the best title.

a Memories are made of this.

b Odours that help in memory loss.

c How do smells help you remember?

P ROOF THAT SMELL IS A POWERFUL MEMORY CUE which can aid the recall of events that occurred more than five years ago finally came after the first research of its kind was published recently.

5   The study, carried out by John Aggleton and Louise Waskett of the University of Wales, involved 45 people who were asked to remember features of the Jorvik Viking Centre in York, which recreates the city during the 10th century using not only sights
10 and sounds but also highly distinctive smells.

The researchers concluded that those participants who were exposed again to the museum's smells could recall their visits more accurately than those who relied on memory alone.

15 Three groups of 15 participants, who had not visited the centre in six years, were given a questionnaire about various displays in the exhibition.

The first group was given a selection of seven odours to sniff, identical to those used at the museum, including 'burnt wood',
20 'apples', 'fish market', and 'rope / tar'.

The control group was given seven different odours not used as part of the exhibition, including coffee, peppermint, coconut and maple. The third group was not given anything to smell.

The results showed exposure to smells present on the last visit
25 to the museum induced a significant improvement in recall.

Professor Aggleton said that smell was a particularly arousing sense because it had the most direct route into the brain regions of all the senses. 'The same brain structures involved in handling smell
30 information are also involved in memory. Smells can also arouse emotions, which affect and modulate memory.' He believes this is the first study to ascertain the accuracy of memory in a real-life situation rather than in laboratory conditions.

Libby Brooks, The Guardian

rise, raise, arise, arouse

1.30 Smells can also arouse emotions

2 Choose the correct highlighted alternative in these sentences.

1 The man's strange behaviour aroused / raised our suspicions, so we called the police

2 Politicians often rise / raise people's expectations with false promises.

3 The new advertising campaign has risen / aroused a lot of interest.

4 The problem has arisen / risen because of the lack of communication between the two groups.

5 The speaker rose / arose to his feet and approached the podium.

The prefix re-

1.2 recall   1.8 recreate

3 In many verbs, nouns, and adjectives beginning with re- , the prefix means *again* or *back*. Complete these sentences with an appropriate word from this list in an appropriate form.

reactivate   readjust   reaffirm   rearrange   retake
recreate   redirect   replace

1 Scott's grades weren't good enough to earn him a university place. He's going to ..*retake*.. his exams and apply again next year.

2 Robert is finding it hard to .... to living in Britain again after being in the States for so long.

3 The film .... the Hollywood of the 1940s.

4 The campaign hopes to .... public concern for the plight of the homeless.

5 She picked up the book, read the back cover then .... it on the shelf.

6 The president .... his intention to cut taxes if he was re-elected.

7 I'm afraid I don't like the way you've .... the furniture. The sofa looked better where it was.

8 When you move house, you can pay to have your mail .... to your new address.

Listening

You are going to hear somebody talking about her earliest memory.

1 Before you listen, think about your **earliest** memory.

2 🎧 **11.2** Listen to the recording once and answer these questions.

1 What was the speaker's earliest memory?

2 How many people were involved?

3 🎧 **11.2** Listen again and answer these questions.

1 Where was the speaker?

2 Where was the speaker's brother?

3 Why did all the water come out of the paddling pool?

4 How did the speaker react when the water went over her face?

Follow up: descriptive verbs

The speaker uses a number of descriptive verbs to make her account more vivid and more interesting.

4 **a** Look at the tapescript on p.86 and find verbs with these meanings.

1 drop or put down heavily or hurriedly (colloquial) ....

2 move on one's hands and knees ....

3 fall over (colloquial) ....

4 flow or pour in large quantities ....

5 make completely wet ....

6 sound made by babies when they are happy ....

b Check your answers then complete these sentences with one of the verbs from 4a in an appropriate form.

1 There was a flash of lightning and then the heavens opened, ... us in seconds.

2 I rarely drink alcohol. One small beer is enough to make me ....

3 Rachel rushed into the kitchen, ... the groceries on the floor, and hurried out again.

4 The soldier .... along the ground cradling his rifle in his arms.

5 Blood .... out of the wound. It was necessary to stem the flow as quickly as possible.

6 Having just been fed, the baby .... contentedly in its cot.

Language focus

used to and *would* SB p.89

1 Complete this extract from a short story with *would* +
an appropriate verb from this list.

arrive   be   count up   get out of   ~~go~~   head off   load up
lose   pull up   ~~spend~~   start   wake up

Family holidays were royal affairs, and most years
we'd *go* ....¹ to Singapore for Christmas.
Mum *would spend* ......² the morning with the
servants, making sandwiches and drinks: we
......................³ the car and then have to wait
for Dad to turn up – he was always late.
We ....⁴ starving because we were
supposed to leave at four to miss the rush hour and
we .... finally ....⁵
the house at about seven, the three of us in the
back seat, Mum and Dad in the front.
We ....⁶ on the 240-mile drive to
Singapore, but the first stop was always Kajang, an
hour from Kuala Lumpur. Kajang had, and
apparently still has, the best satay* in Malaysia.

We ....⁷ the city lights pretty quickly,
drive through rubber estates, and then over this
particular crest and on the horizon we could see

a neon glow. Kajang! Our stomach juices
......................⁸ flowing, we could practically
smell the satay in the air. Finally we ....
⁹ and run inside, and we used to eat forty satay sticks
each. They ....¹⁰ the sticks, that's how
they charged. Then we'd collapse back in the car and
Dad would drive the rest of the night to Singapore.
We ....¹¹ around two in the morning
and be carried, bleary-eyed, into Aunty Pari's house
and put to bed. The next morning we
......................¹² to the sound of traffic on
Clemenceau Avenue, just off Orchard Road.

Places in the Heart, Pria Viswalingam

* **satay:** small pieces of meat grilled on a skewer and served
  with a spicy sauce.

2 Correct any mistakes in the highlighted parts of
these sentences.

1 When I was young we would always have a three-
course meal for Sunday lunch.

2 When I was a kid, we used to play outside till all hours.
We'd go home when we felt hungry.

3 At first I found it really strange but now I am used to eat
my evening meal at 10 p.m.

4 I hardly ever cook these days but I would be a good
cook. My speciality was roast lamb.

5 A Before we had this restaurant we would own one
in Oxford.

   B Would you really?

6 You usen't to be a vegetarian, used you?

7 Up until a few years ago my mother was always baking.
She would bake her own bread and biscuits.

8 I used not to like fast food but I don't eat anything else
these days.

Omitting words SB p.91

3 Read these short dialogues and cross out any unnecessary words in B's replies.

1 A Would you like to come round for lunch tomorrow?

   B I'd love to ~~come round for lunch tomorrow~~. What time ~~would you like me to come round for lunch tomorrow~~?

2 A Have you lived here long?

   B Yes, I have lived here long.

3 A Ask Nick if he'd like to come with us.

   B I will ask Nick if he'd like to come with us.

4 A What kind of books do you read?

   B I read autobiographies, I read the classics, and I read poetry.

5 A Have you seen this film before?

   B I have seen this film many times.

🎧 **12.1** Listen and check.

HAVE YOU SEEN THIS FILM BEFORE??

4 Write in the words or phrases which have been left out in these informal dialogues.

1 A What's wrong with you? You look a bit pale.

   B Headache. My own fault. Shouldn't have drunk that wine.

2 A This yours?

   B No. Might be John's.

   A This your watch, John?

   C Wouldn't be seen dead wearing a watch like that!

3 A Hungry? Fancy something to eat?

   B You offering to cook something?

4 A Nice to meet you.

   B Nice of you to invite me.

5 A Read any good books lately?

   B One or two. You?

Vocabulary focus

Phrasal verbs with *off* SB p.93

1 Complete these sentences with an appropriate phrasal verb from this list in an appropriate form.

block off   break off   call off   divide off   kick off   set off
spark off

1 The spy plane incident almost .... a war between the two countries.

2 The cup final is due to .... at 8 p.m.

3 If we don't want to miss the beginning of the film we'd better .... now.

4 The police .... the main exits to the building so that the robbers couldn't escape.

5 In the restaurant the no-smoking area is clearly .... from the smoking section.

6 David and Sandra can't seem to agree on where to get married. David wants a registry office wedding but Sandra is threatening to .... the whole thing .... if they don't get married in church.

7 The United States say they will .... diplomatic relations with the country concerned unless the hostages are returned safely.

2 Choose the correct highlighted phrasal verb in these sentences.

1 Most of the action takes place in the main square and the roads leading off / taking off it.

2 Filming had to be taken off / put off for several hours until the storm had passed.

3 The 'Fasten your seatbelt' sign will come on before the plane takes off / leads off.

4 At the end of the film the newly-married couple wave off / drive off into the sunset in a pink Cadillac.

5 Before filming could start, the streets around the cathedral had to be closed off / taken off to traffic.

6 We'll come to the station to put you off / wave you off.

7 I phoned Peter the other day to tell him I had a cinema ticket going spare, but he closed off / rang off before I had the chance.

Vocabulary expansion

1 **a** Before you read this magazine article about boomerangs, see how much you know.

    1 Boomerangs were originally used for
      a attacking the enemy
      b sending messages
      c hunting animals

    2 Boomerangs are traditionally made of
      a metal
      b wood
      c stone

    3 Boomerangs should be thrown
      a into the wind
      b towards the sun
      c from the shoulder

   b Read the article and check your answers.

What a comeback

Watch out; boomerangs are back. No pun intended. The resurgence of the sport appeals to my inherent laziness – for once you've thrown a boomerang, you can remain rooted to the spot and it will return to you. No more running after the frisbee or 5 hunting for a lost ball. I just needed a lesson.

My brother advised me: 'Put some effort into it. Flick your wrist. Look after your fingernails.' But his main observation was that I 'throw like a girl'. I'd be in for a hard time. Wooden, banana-shaped and rather heavy, his boomerang 10 was the real thing, handmade by aborigines in the traditional manner. Thousands of years ago, the boomerang was an ideal weapon: if the thrower missed his target, the missile would return to him; if he made a hit, he got lunch.

In retrospect, I think my brother's boomerang was supposed to 15 be ornamental. After hours of practice, it didn't come back to us once. So it was not with confidence that I met up with boomerang maestro David Strang for my lesson. I brightened up, however, when he told me that his 'Rangs' are guaranteed to return when thrown as directed, that kids as young as eight are 20 great at it, and that I'd be proficient after half an hour.

David went over the technique several times: face the wind, turn 45 degrees to the right of it, keep the boomerang vertical and hurl it straight to the horizon. I chucked it as hard as I could. After 25 a dozen or so poor throws, my elbow was hurting but so was my pride. David's encouragement kept me going. I want to get better at it. I want to prove that it's 30 not just a boy thing.

Viki Reeve, Evening Standard Magazine

Verbs like *throw*

1.7 *flick*   **1.25** *chuck*

2 **a** Look at these verbs which describe different ways of throwing and match them with their meanings.

    1 ☐ Chuck me that newspaper, will you?
    2 ☐ Chris tossed a coin to see who should go first.
    3 ☐ She flicked the mosquito off her hand.
    4 ☐ They heaved the boulder over the cliff.

    a use thumb and finger to propel something small and light with a quick action
    b (informal) throw something in a careless or relaxed way
    c throw or lift something heavy using a lot of effort
    d throw in the air so that it turns; throw something, usually light, with a quick movement of the hand; move or make move from side to side or up and down

  b Check your answers then complete each group of sentences with one verb from 2a in the appropriate form.

    1 When you've finished with that magazine, just _chuck_ it away.

      Chuck me over those keys, will you?

    2 Can you try not to .... ash on the carpet?

      She .... the hair out of her eyes.

    3 In tug-of-war each side holds onto one end of the rope and then .... as hard as they can.

      It took four burly men to .... the heavy wardrobe up the stairs.

    4 The children .... bread to the ducks which were swimming in the lake.

      The small boat .... up and down by the huge waves.

      I couldn't sleep. I .... and turned all night.

Idioms with *back*

3 a Do you think the following statements are True or False?

1 ☐ If something or somebody is back or makes a comeback , they become popular again.

2 ☐ If you live in the back of beyond , you live in a busy town or city where there is a lot going on.

3 ☐ If someone puts your back up , they annoy you.

4 ☐ If you wear your sweater back to front you will look stupid.

5 ☐ If you are a back-seat driver you drive the car sitting in the back seat.

b Check your answers then complete the gaps with the most appropriate idiom from 3a.

1970s flares   21st century flares

1 Nowadays with computer technology you could live ...., miles from anywhere and still work for an international company.

2 Did you get dressed in the dark this morning? You're wearing your pullover inside out and ....

3 The sort of things that really .... are: people shouting into mobile phones in restaurants, people talking behind my back, and people lighting up after a meal without asking you if you mind.

4 Flares, which first came on the fashion scene in the 1960s, ... in the 1990s.

5 My Aunt Julia is a typical .... It's so hard to concentrate when she's shouting out things like, 'Look out! You're going to hit that car!'

Listening

You are going to hear three people talking about what they were interested in when they were young.

1 🎧 **12.2** Listen to each recording once and decide what each speaker is talking about.

Speaker 1
a a pet
b a soft toy
c a doll

Speaker 2
a a rock garden
b rock music
c a rock collection

Speaker 3
a playing tricks on people
b performing in public
c doing magic

2 🎧 **12.2** Listen again and decide whether these sentences are True or False.

Speaker 1
1 ☐ The speaker threw Brownie in the waste basket because he didn't love him any more.
2 ☐ The speaker cut off Brownie's nose.

Speaker 2
1 ☐ The speaker probably has rocks from all over the USA.
2 ☐ She labelled them all and gave them names.

Speaker 3
1 ☐ The speaker's parents didn't know about his interest.
2 ☐ He didn't like performing in front of his friends.

Follow up: American words and idioms

3 Look at the tapescript on p.86 and find American words and expressions for their British equivalents below.

Speaker 1
angry with   ....
I'll show you   ....

Speaker 2
child   ....
I suppose   ....
hell   ....

Speaker 3
parents   ....
the town centre   ....
meanie   ....

13

Language focus

-ing forms SB p.99

1 Complete this extract from a novel with one of these
-ing forms. Some are nouns, some are verbs, and some
are adjectives.

distracting	floating	leaning	looking out	reaching
reassuring	shouting	standing	starting	wiping

Heat. It had touched Sean that afternoon as he sat on
Manila Bay's low harbour wall, ... ¹ at the cargo
ships and their fat anchor chains. Up to then he'd been
protected by the .... ² air-con of an Ermita
McDonald's. He'd gone there for breakfast, around
ten a.m, with a copy of *Asia Week* rolled in his fist. At
eleven fifteen he'd stood up to leave and walked towards
the exit, where the blue-uniformed McDonald's security
guard had obligingly lowered his stockless shot-gun and
held the door open. Or obligingly held the door open
and lowered his stockless shotgun. Either way, one blast
from the scorched air and Sean had spun on his heels and
marched back inside.

But cool as it was in McDonald's, after a couple of hours
Sean could feel the edges of his mind .... ³ to fray.
It wasn't the obsessive ashtray-removing and washing
and .... ⁴ so much as the sprawling children's party
that had commandeered half the seating area.
Overweight rich kids with sulky faces and stripy sailors'
shirts, ... ⁵ at their nannies. Why did this tubby
elite choose to celebrate in a hamburger joint, Sean had
wondered as he burst a balloon that had been bounced
into his face. The sound made a dozen adult heads turn

adjective + preposition + -ing form

2 Choose the correct highlighted preposition in these
sentences.

1 If you are fed up at / with people pushing you around,
do something about it.

2 Some people are afraid of / with losing their jobs, which
is why they put up with bullying.

3 I must admit I'm not very good in / at confronting people.

4 Most of us are guilty of / at flying off the handle
if somebody does something to annoy us.

5 Avoiding conflict is different from / in behaving in
a cowardly way.

6 What's wrong with / about apologizing to someone
if you do something wrong?

7 Tony was ashamed at / of having spoken to Jane so
harshly and said he was sorry.

8 Would you be interested in / on doing an assertiveness
course?

🎧 13.1 Listen, check, and repeat.

and had one of the minders .... ⁶ under his *barong
tagalog* to the bulge in his waistband. So, time to go.

Armed with a milkshake, Sean had left the McDonald's
and walked to the waterfront, where he'd hoped he might
kill time in the company of a cool sea breeze. There was
an executive-bathroom hand-drier blowing down his
neck. The milkshake had turned to chocolate soup before
it was even a quarter finished, the bench he'd chosen
was like .... ⁷ against an oven door, and the sparse
canopies of the palm trees offered nothing more than a
rumour of shade. Yet somehow Sean had managed to
stick it out until four. He couldn't remember much about
how the time had passed, he was simply glad that it had.
Ships and water were good for .... ⁸ a head that
needed to be distracted. Good for a blink and a mild
frown, and a glance at a watch that said half an hour had
swept by. Sean's only clear memory of the afternoon was
.... ⁹ on the harbour wall and looking down at the
beached jellyfish and acres of .... ¹⁰ refuse.

The Tesseract, Alex Garland

verb + (object +) preposition + -ing form SB p.99

3 a Check that you know which prepositions are used with these verbs.

1 accuse somebody ....

2 admit ....

3 agree ....

4 believe ....

5 blame somebody ....

6 complain ....

7 depend ....

8 discourage somebody ....

9 rely ....

10 stop somebody ....

11 use something ....

12 worry ....

b Rewrite these sentences using a verb and preposition from 3a and an appropriate -ing form. Some sentences will need an object.

1 It's your fault the ornament got broken, Tom. You dropped it!

Paul ....
the ornament.

2 It must have been Craig who stole the exam paper. He was the only person in the room at the time.

She ....
the exam paper.

3 Don't admit responsibility for the accident, Jacob, whatever you do.

Jacob's brother ....
responsibility for the accident.

4 I don't think people should be kept in prison for life.

I don't ....
in prison for life.

5 Don't you know what a colander is? You drain water from vegetables with it – after they're cooked.

A colander ....
water from vegetables after they're cooked.

6 All right. It was my fault. I was the one who left the front door open.

Gary ....
the front door open.

7 This train is always late! I've had enough and I'm going to talk to someone about it.

Beth is going to ....
late.

8 It was lucky I was wearing my seatbelt. I would have been thrown forward when I braked otherwise.

Luke's seatbelt ....
when he braked.

Singular or plural? SB p.101

4 Correct any mistakes in the verb or pronoun forms in these sentences.

1 Mathematics are a compulsory subject in schools.

2 The family that live next door to my sister have decided to emigrate to Australia. They think there will be better job prospects there.

3 Not one of the students has handed in their homework.

4 The average British family have 2.4 children.

5 There's people in my class who speak several languages.

6 The government plans to put back the elections.

7 The early evening news are on at six o'clock.

8 Karl is one of the few people I know who have never been abroad.

9 Although England hasn't won the World Cup since 1966, they have a fair chance of winning this time.

10 A number of people has complained about the facilities.

11 Every team which takes part gets a prize. Last year's winning team are hoping to be successful once more.

12 The police has issued a statement about the incident.

Vocabulary focus

Conflict: collocations SB p.102

1 Choose the correct highlighted alternative in these sentences.

1 What started off as a minor incident escalated into a serious / full-scale war.

2 The conflict will never be won / resolved until both sides agree to sit down and talk.

3 The bitter / sharp quarrel over which parent should have custody of the children dragged on for months before it was finally settled by the courts.

4 There is pitched / fierce disagreement between the main political parties on issues of law and order.

5 There is a difference between a heated discussion and a blazing / sharp row.

6 After lengthy discussions unions and management reached / created a compromise on pay.

7 The row was created / sparked off by a stupid misunderstanding.

8 A / an armed / pitched battle erupted between both sets of supporters when the match ended in a goalless draw.

9 The army quelled / resolved the rebellion, arresting the main ringleaders.

10 The battle was resolved / won but the war was lost / crushed.

Conflict: idioms SB p.102

2 a Here are some idioms related to the topic of conflict. Do you think these statements are True or False?

1 ☐ If two people are at each other's throats they are arguing.

2 ☐ If someone accuses you of splitting hairs they think you are being aggressive.

3 ☐ If you have a bone to pick with someone you are annoyed with them about something they have or haven't done.

4 ☐ If you bury the hatchet you forget your argument with someone and make peace.

5 ☐ If you say something which clears the air you make a conflictive situation worse.

6 ☐ If Rita and Sally settle their differences they disagree with each other.

b Match the sentences and sentence beginnings 1–5 with the best continuations a–e.

1 ☐ I've got a bone to pick with you.

2 ☐ Perhaps I'm splitting hairs

3 ☐ It's better to say what you think and clear the air

4 ☐ It's high time they buried the hatchet.

5 ☐ We've agreed to settle our differences.

a They haven't talked to each other since they fell out five years ago.

b We've both apologized and agreed to forget about the whole thing.

c That book I lent you has got some pages missing.

d but I do think there is a difference between bullying and harassment.

e than keep things bottled up.

Vocabulary expansion

1 Read this extract from a novel and decide whether these statements are True or False.

1 ☐ The arguments are always about the same thing.
2 ☐ The author's grandmother stands up to her daughter and argues with her.
3 ☐ The grandmother usually wins the arguments.

T HAT'S how it is in our house these days. Fights start out of the blue and this time it's all because of poor Seepie, who in my mother's eyes can do no wrong.

5 You have to watch out for my mother. My grandmother says she's never known a woman get so worked up as my mother does and about such funny things and living in our house these days is like walking on thin ice
10 every day of your life but all the same my grandmother has never in her life learned not to say exactly what she wants to say to a daughter who gets too big for her boots.

'You've got it all worked out,' she says. 'And a
15 big mouth to tell it with.'

'Leave it alone, Ma,' says my mother and she makes as if she's tired and has had enough and is going to get up and go out for a walk but my grandmother says she can sit right where she is
20 and hear her out.

I think there'll be another fight but there isn't. My mother just looks at my grandmother and shakes her head.

You can see how fed up she is. She pushes her
25 chair back so it nearly falls over and gets up from the table. She looks for her cardigan and purse and says she's had enough for one day, she's going out for a breath of air and she throws her cardigan over her shoulders as if
30 she's going to the front door but I know her by now. She won't leave without having the last word because that isn't her way.

Pamela Jooste, Dance with a Poor Man's Daughter

Idioms with *big*

1.13 *too big for her boots*

2 Choose the correct highlighted alternative in these idioms.

1 My dream is to go to Hollywood and make / do it big in the movie business.
2 Patrick always orders too much food when we go out to a restaurant. His nose is / eyes are bigger than his belly.
3 Let's give a big palm / hand to the treasurer in appreciation for all the work he has done.
4 Jim has decided to leave the multinational he works for and go to a smaller company. He'd rather be a big frog / fish in a little pond.
5 Don't worry about it. It's no big problem / deal.
6 Ignore the details for the moment. Just try to see the bigger picture / image.

Idioms with *word / words*

1.31 *having the last word*

3 Choose the correct highlighted alternative in these idioms.

1 Tom was as good / reliable as his word and was at the station to meet me as promised.
2 Freda complained that she hadn't said what she had been reported to have said. The journalist had dropped / put words in her mouth.
3 It's a secret so don't breathe / whisper a word to anyone, will you?
4 A Mr James called me into his office and told me that I would need to pull up my socks or else. He said I was untidy, unpunctual, and lazy.
   B He doesn't cut up / mince his words, does he?
5 A Can I borrow the car this weekend, Dad?
   B In / With a word, no.
6 I've enjoyed this project, right from the word go / start.

Listening

1 🎧 **13.2** Listen to the recording once and answer these questions.

1 Who is the woman?
  a a colleague of Bill's
  b Bill's boss
  c an employee of Bill's
2 Who has the problem?
  a Bill
  b both Bill and the woman
  c another person in the company

2 Match the highlighted words and phrases from the recording with their meanings.

1 ☐ *You kind of* imply …
2 ☐ *I am* committed …
3 ☐ *… a case of* passing the buck …
4 ☐ *… falls within my* jurisdiction …
5 ☐ *… the* heart of the matter …

a caring a lot about one's job
b authority to make and deal with decisions
c most important thing
d suggest indirectly
e transfer the responsibility or blame for something to somebody else

3 🎧 **13.2** Listen again and decide whether the following statements are True or False.

1 ☐ The woman questions Bill's devotion to the company.
2 ☐ Bill is not clear what his responsibilities are.
3 ☐ The woman is sympathetic to Bill's situation.
4 ☐ The woman feels Bill should talk to her if he has a problem.
5 ☐ Bill feels the situation is rather unfair.

Follow up: weak forms

Auxiliary verbs, modal verbs, personal pronouns, and several prepositions have weak and strong forms, for example:

> *Who's he staring* **at**? (æt)
>
> *I think he's staring* **at** *you.* (ət)

We use the strong forms of these words when we want to stress them. Otherwise we use the weak forms.

4 a Look at these extracts from the recording. Decide whether you think the highlighted words were used in their strong or their weak form. Why do you think the strong were forms used?

1 *It's a bit unfair because* you know you *say* that *this doesn't get done.*
2 *… there's there's so much* that *isn't made clear to* me .
3 *… everyone else is in* the *same position as* you ?
4 I'm *sorry but if other people* are *coping with this situation I don't see why it's so difficult for* you .
5 *And if you* do *have a problem then talk* to *somebody about it.*
6 *This is really the heart of the matter – that* you *feel that* we're *always blaming* you .

b 🎧 **13.3** Listen and see if you were right.

14

Language focus

Ability and possibility `SB p.105`

1 Complete these sentences with an appropriate form of *can*, *could*, *be able to*, *manage*, *succeed*. You will sometimes need to use the negative.

1 Jane still .... in finding a job as good as her last one, but she says she'll keep looking.

2 You .... get into trouble if you send personal e-mails during office time.

3 I'm sorry I .... attend to your enquiry personally when you called yesterday. I was out of the office at the time.

4 A Bruce hasn't a hope in hell of getting that job.
   B I don't know. He .... be just what they're looking for.

5 I didn't really want to attend the seminar and I .... gone anyway as I'd already booked my holidays for those dates

6 Margaret sent off over two hundred job applications before she finally .... get a job.

7 The company regrets that it .... give refunds without a receipt.

8 I .... contact him more quickly if he'd had e-mail.

9 Kurt is very ambitious. After only six months with the firm he .... get himself promoted.

10 The advertising campaign .... certainly .... in raising the profile of our product.

11 I .... never .... understand why they didn't give the post to Adrian.

12 .... you understand what these figures mean? You can? Great, because I .... and I've got to type up a summary for the managing director.

13 Hopefully, the new directors .... turn things round and make the company profitable once more.

14 If I .... attend the conference, I would have, but the dates were impossible.

Indefinite pronouns `SB p.107`

2 Choose the correct highlighted alternative in these sentences.

1 Could no one / someone open this bottle for me?

2 Anybody / Everybody knows it was Douglas and not me who spilt the wine on the carpet. Ask anyone / everyone . They'll vouch for me.

3 I haven't got enough time to send out the invitations. Anybody / Somebody else will have to do it.

4 Everybody / Nobody said how much they'd enjoyed the party. It was one of the best they'd been to in a long time.

5 Could you tell Russell to turn the music down? He pays no attention to anything / nothing I say.

6 Eliza knew that something / everything wasn't right when she opened the door. It was too quiet. Then she heard anyone / someone shout 'Surprise!'.

7 Amelia found nothing / everything about her husband irritating. She therefore found it ironic that they were celebrating their twentieth wedding anniversary. What particularly irritated her was when he said, 'Well, no one / anyone is perfect'.

8 Thinking she had heard the doorbell, Lucy went to open the door but there wasn't nobody / anybody there.

9 Would anyone / someone like another sandwich?

10 A Are you coming to the party?
   B Somebody / Nobody told me there was a party.
   A Oh, sorry. Haven't you been invited?

3 Complete this extract from a novel with a word from this list.

all (X3)   everybody   everyone   nobody   no one

It was on one such night that I had a strange dream. There was a large gathering of well-dressed people .... ¹ attending a somewhat formal party in what appeared to be a hotel. Waitresses in black-and-white uniforms floated among the gathering with trays of drinks and light snacks. The one thing that .... ² had in common was that I knew them .... ³, but .... ⁴ was paying any attention to me. I couldn't understand what was going on, so I took one of the waitresses aside and asked her who the party was for. She looked at me with genuine surprise and said, 'Don't you know?' I assured her I didn't have the slightest idea and asked her again. 'It's for you,' she said.

I still couldn't understand it – the formal dress, the subdued atmosphere, the drinks and the food. 'What kind of party is it?' I asked.

She was now getting irritated with me. 'Are you sure you don't know?' She paused for a moment before saying, 'It's a funeral.'

I woke up instantly. Every detail of the dream was vivid and the logic of it was simple – .... ⁵ knowing me, but not .... ⁶ knowing each other, and .... ⁷ paying any attention to me because I wasn't really there.

John Beattie, The Breath of Angels

Vocabulary focus

The prefix co- SB p.104

1 The prefix *co-* often means 'together'. Complete these sentences with an appropriate *co-* word from this list.

coalition   coexistence   cohesion   coincidence
collaboration   collocation   co-operation

1 This piece of writing has no .... It just doesn't hold together as a text.
2 It was no .... you met Adam there. He knew you were going.
3 'Heavy' is a .... of rain whereas 'strong' isn't.
4 We could not have done it without your .... Thank you so much for all your help.
5 One wonders whether the countries of the world will ever be able to live in peaceful ....
6 No political party won outright so there will have to be a ....
7 The police worked in close .... with members of the community on the project.

Phrasal verbs with *out* SB p.107

2 Complete these sentences with an appropriate verb from this list in an appropriate form.

cut   die   go   lock   run   share

1 The profits are .... out equally among the partners.
2 Jason came home earlier than expected from his round-the-world trip because he .... out of money.
3 I always leave a set of keys with a neighbour in case I .... myself out.
4 It's no good smoking fewer cigarettes. You have to .... them out altogether.
5 Unless something is done about the deforestation problem, many species .... out in the coming years.
6 It was freezing in the room. Richard had forgotten to put more logs on the fire and it .... out.

🎧 **14.1** Listen, check, and repeat.

Vocabulary expansion

1

a Before you read this extract from a newspaper article about time, which alternative do you think is true in each of these statements?

1 Compared with fifty years ago people are working more / fewer hours.

2 People feel under less / more pressure nowadays.

3 Time management is a more / less important feature of life today.

b Read the extract and see if the writer agrees with you.

Fast forward

A survey published today suggests that people are working ever harder and longer. Isn't it time we learnt to clock off?

5 Time is running out. Or so people feel. According to the latest research, 44% of British workers come home exhausted. More than half suffer from stress. By almost every measure, people are more pressured, more bothered about time – or a lack of it – than they have been for many years.

10 Right across the West the old ways of managing time are disappearing. Fixed jobs, shared rhythms of shopping, travel and leisure, and common patterns of learning, marriage and retirement are all on the way out. Instead the world is having to

15 come to terms with just-in-time production and multi-tasking computers, 24-hour shopping and video-on-demand, time-share holidays and flexi-time working, late opening at schools and home banking. All of these are symptoms of a revolution,

20 a transition from an industrial time culture based around fixed timetables and a clear division of labour between men who want to work and women who looked after the home, towards a new culture based around flexibility, customisation, and rapid

25 flows of information.

Demos Quarterly

Expressions with *time*

1.4 *Time is running out.*

2

a Here are some more common expressions with *time*. Do you think the following sentences are True or False?

1 ☐ If somebody arrives on time, they are punctual.

2 ☐ If someone plays for time, they try to gain time by delaying.

3 ☐ If you take your time, you do things as quickly as you can.

4 ☐ If you say you are going to change jobs and your friend says 'Not before time', they think you should have changed jobs a long time ago.

5 ☐ If you are going to stay in your job for the time being, you do not intend to change jobs soon.

b Complete these sentences with an appropriate time expression from 2a.

1 A I hear Rob's getting married.

B .... They've been dating for 15 years!

2 We're not in any hurry so just ....

3 Ian is never .... I get fed up waiting for him.

4 The most common way of .... when someone phones up asking for immediate payment of a bill is to say, 'The cheque is in the post.'

5 A Are you planning to move house once the baby's born?

B No we'll stay where we are ....

Expressions with *come*

1.15 *come to terms with*

3 Complete these expressions with a word from this list.

clean   crunch   earth   handy   terms

1 Don't throw that old shirt away. It might come in .... for something.

2 Courtney is finding it hard to come to .... with being a single woman again after having been married for so long.

3 The burglar decided to come .... and admitted a number of other offences.

4 Karen came down to .... with a bang when she realized she didn't have the grades she needed to study medicine.

5 Greg always says he'll give us a hand but when it comes to the .... he's always too busy.

Listening

You are going to hear Tony talking about the career he would follow if he had the opportunity.

1 **Before you listen, answer these questions about yourself, depending on your situation.**

   If you haven't started a career yet

   a What career do you plan to take up and why?

   b What drawbacks might there be?

   If you are already working

   a What career would you follow if you had the chance and why?

   b What drawbacks might there be?

2 🎧 **14.2** **Listen to the recording once and answer these questions.**

   1 What careers would the speaker choose and why?

   2 What drawbacks would there be?

3 🎧 **14.2** **Listen again and answer these questions.**

   1 What specialism would Tony choose?

   2 What specialism wouldn't he choose and why?

   3 What would most concern him about his choice of career?

4 **Look at the tapescript on p.87 and choose the best meaning for the highlighted words.**

   1 *Surgery has always* intrigued *me …*
      a amazed
      b fascinated
      c interested

   2 *I love* tinkering with *machines …*
      a playing
      b constructing
      c trying to repair

   3 *You* can't afford *to make mistakes.*
      a it will cause problems if you do this
      b it will be expensive if you do this
      c it will be irresponsible to do this

   4 *… eyes are* squishy and squashy.
      a horrible to both touch and look at
      b soft and easily crushed
      c complex and easily damaged

Follow up: pauses in speech

> When we speak, we divide what we want to say into chunks.
>
> If we are trying to present a reasoned argument, we may divide the information into smaller chunks and have longer pauses in between them than normal.
>
> This gives us more time to think of exactly what we want to say.

5 a **Look at these extracts from the recording and decide where the appropriate places for the speaker to pause would be. The number of actual pauses the speaker makes is in brackets.**

   1 *If I really had a choice then I'd definitely change em and I think there are two possibilities two things I really would like to do and which I've always wanted to do …(6)*

   2 *… engineering has always intrigued me the way things are built and the way things work er machines I love machines I love tinkering with machines and in a way the human body is is something like that. (6)*

   3 *You've got all the various systems in the body and you've got all the various things like the bones and the various organs and it would be fascinating I think trying to repair this system. (6)*

   b 🎧 **14.3** **Listen and check your answers.**

15

Language focus

Alternatives to relative clauses SB p.111

1 Which relative clauses have been omitted from these newspaper extracts?

a

Stormy cruise ends happily

A man and two teenage boys, *who were* found after 24 hours adrift in their small boat in the North Sea, are lucky to be alive. Cleveland police said that Jack Gibson, 38, his son Derek, and his friend Timothy, both 15, were spotted by the crew of an aircraft patrolling in the area. The three, all from Lingdale, Cleveland were airlifted to Middlesborough General Hospital, suffering from mild exposure.

Daily Express

b

Bug beating car thieves

Cars fitted with electronic bugs are helping police to catch big-time thieves. The cars, parked in areas with a high theft rate, lead police to the heart of car-crime operations when they are stolen. The system has led to the recovery of vehicles worth more than £500,000 this year. One raid found 13 Porsches and Jaguars hidden in a secret hideaway.

Daily Express

2 Remove any unnecessary relative clauses in this newspaper report.

Bungling burglars let down by overloaded lift

Detectives, ~~who were~~ called to a shop which is in Southend, Essex early yesterday morning, found two burglars who were stuck in a lift with the office safe. Alerted when people who were leaving a discotheque which is next door had heard shouts for help and banging from Spoils, which is in the High Street, the police found that the offices, which are above, had been ransacked.

In their haste to get away, two men, who are both in their 20s, had tried to take a heavy office safe downstairs in a small service lift. They did not notice a sign on the door which warned that it was meant for no more than two people. It stuck between floors because they overloaded it. The two burglars had been trying to attract attention for most of the six hours they were locked in, but it was not until the Club Arts disco, which is next door, closed its Christmas Eve special that anyone heard them. They could easily have stayed there over Christmas until the staff who work in Spoils came in again on Tuesday morning. The burglars, who had hoped the safe would be their Christmas present, said they had never been so pleased to see police and firemen in their lives.

The Times

Fronting SB p.113

3 Rewrite these sentences in a more 'normal' order.

1 Impatiently, he tore open the envelope and hurriedly scanned its contents.
   He tore open the envelope impatiently and scanned its ....
   contents hurriedly. ....

2 Usually for breakfast I just have a black coffee.
   ....

3 Fried eggs I love, but scrambled eggs I loathe.
   ....

4 In the centre of the old part of the town stands the cathedral.
   ....

5 Shopping on a Saturday afternoon; I absolutely detest it.
   ....

6 Not in a million years would I have guessed the answer.
   ....

7 Never did I imagine she wasn't telling the truth.
   ....

8 Driving in the dark I find difficult.
   ....

-ing forms and infinitives `SB p.115`

4 Correct any mistakes in the highlighted verb forms.

1 You don't need ~~explaining~~ what you were doing. I know exactly what you were doing. *to explain*

2 I had written the answers on a small piece of paper but unfortunately I forgot taking it into the exam room.

3 Sit so I can see over your shoulder.

4 I'm hopeless at cheat . I always get found out.

5 It's nerve-wracking to cheat in an exam.

6 I'll never forget to be found out . I was embarrassed and worried about the consequences at the same time.

7 The use of identity cards in exams helps prevent people cheating .

8 I'm looking forward to the test be over , aren't you?

5 Choose the correct highlighted alternative in these sentences.

1 I meant to tell / telling you that we couldn't come on Saturday. Sorry, I forgot.

2 I don't remember to offer / offering to baby-sit tonight but it isn't a problem.

3 I wonder if Gina regrets to get / getting married so young.

4 If he goes on to spend / spending money at that rate, he'll soon run out.

5 After they'd been digging for twenty minutes they stopped to have / having a rest.

6 Dr Lee regrets to inform / informing patients that he cannot see anyone without an appointment.

7 Trevor asked me how I was but before I could reply he went on to tell / telling me all about his bad back.

8 Having children means to make / making a lot of sacrifices but most people think it's worth it.

9 You will remember to post / posting that letter, won't you?

10 A I'm trying to lose / losing weight so I've stopped to have / having breakfast.

   B Have you tried to join / joining a slimming club?

🎧 **15.1** Listen, check, and repeat.

Verbs of perception `Language commentary p.117`

6 Complete the text with an appropriate verb in the appropriate form – infinitive without *to* or *-ing*.

I woke at 5 a.m. Something must have woken me up because I had been fast asleep. At first I could hear nothing – only an occasional car .... [1] past on the street and a dog .... [2]. Then I became aware of angry voices coming from the flat above. I heard a man's voice .... [3] angrily, 'How could you? You're no daughter of mine! Get out!' and a door .... [4] loudly a few minutes later. Curious, I got out of bed and went over to the window. The street was empty but after a few minutes I saw the door below .... [5] and a young woman .... [6] the building carrying a small suitcase. A taxi drew up outside the block of flats and I watched the driver .... [7] of his cab and .... [8] her suitcase in the boot. She climbed into the back seat, lit a cigarette and gave directions to the driver. As the taxi was leaving she glanced up and saw me .... [9] at her. Had she been hoping someone else would be looking down?

Vocabulary focus

The prefix *out-* SB p.110

She outscreamed a male rival

1 **a Look at these three meanings of the prefix *out*. Use the example sentences below to help you write the highlighted words in the appropriate column.**

greater or better than	separate from; isolated	showing shock or disapproval

1 I wouldn't want to live in the Australian outback. I'd rather live on the coastal strip.

2 Bernie has shot up in the last year and has outgrown all his clothes.

3 Each competitor has to outdo the others by lifting a heavier weight.

4 The price we have to pay for petrol nowadays is absolutely outrageous.

5 The estate comprises a large house and several outbuildings including a stable and barn.

6 The thief has always managed to outwit the police, and so far has never been caught.

7 Although we've lived here for twenty years, we're still treated as outsiders.

8 His hairstyle can only be described as outlandish. Short on one side and long on the other. I've never seen anything like it!

b Complete these sentences with an appropriate *out*-word from 1a making any necessary changes to form.

1 He behaved .... at the wedding reception. He got very drunk and insulted everyone.

2 Ali has .... all his toys. He says they are childish and that he wants a computer.

3 .... have a very glamorous view of what it's like to work on television.

4 It is difficult to .... computer hackers. They are always one step ahead of everyone else.

5 Surprisingly, Jonathan .... everyone else and came top of his class.

6 The groom had on a rather .... outfit. He looked more like an artist than someone about to be married.

7 The fire started in the farmhouse and spread to nearby ....

Vocabulary expansion

1 **Before you read this extract from a novel, answer these questions truthfully about yourself.**

1 What sort of things do you lie about?

2 Why do you lie?

2 **Read the extract and find out why the author thinks some people lie.**

Some people like secrets: they love knowing things that other people don't know. They specially like knowing things that other people need to know and not telling them. They like to lead people on in their ignorance, sniggering at them inside. There are men and women   5
who only really enjoy a relationship if it's a guilty secret. There are others who love to hear the betrayed spouse defending a treacherous partner. There are people who cannot answer the phone without lying; 'Just a minute. I'll see if she's in', they say, looking 'her' right in the eye.   10
There are people who mime in the presence of the blind. Our whole lives are lived in a tangle of telling, not telling, misleading, allowing to know, concealing, eavesdropping and collusion. When Washington said he could not tell a lie, his father must have answered, 'You had better learn.'   15

Daddy We Hardly Knew You, Germaine Greer

Dishonesty: words and expressions

3 **a Do you think these sentences are True or False?**

1 ☐ If you were misled by a picture in a holiday brochure you were expecting something different.

2 ☐ If you eavesdrop you find out information about someone by secretly opening their mail.

3 ☐ If you conceal information you tell it to people.

4 ☐ If someone leads you up the garden path they are trying to sell you their house.

5 ☐ If a woman accuses a man of leading her on, he possibly gave her the impression that he was interested in marrying her when he had no intention of doing so.

6 ☐ If you collude in doing something, you work secretly with someone else.

b Check your answers then complete these sentences with an appropriate word or phrase from 3a in the appropriate form.

1 I caught Nigel .... outside the door.

2 Some women try to .... their age by dressing younger.

3 The photograph in this catalogue is .... It makes the tent look quite large when I know for a fact that it's quite small.

4 Alice accused Darryl of .... Apparently he hadn't mentioned the fact that he was married.

5 Sometimes the police .... with small-time criminals to catch more important criminals.

6 He .... He told her the roof needed repairing, which it didn't, asked her to pay up front, and then disappeared with the money.

Ways of laughing

1.5 *sniggering*

4 **a** Look at these verbs and their definitions.

cackle:	laugh in a loud unpleasant way, like a chicken that has just laid an egg
chuckle:	laugh quietly, often to oneself
giggle:	laugh in a silly or nervous way, like children
snigger:	laugh in a low unpleasant way, especially at something rude, or at someone else's troubles
titter:	give a short nervous laugh, often of embarrassment

b Choose the more appropriate highlighted alternative in these sentences.

1 The two eighty-year-olds cackled / giggled like schoolgirls as they recalled the pranks they had played on their teacher.

2 Robert opened the paper at the cartoons and spent the next few minutes chuckling / sniggering quietly to himself.

3 'I'll get my own back! You wait and see if I don't!' the old woman tittered / cackled .

4 The audience chuckled / tittered nervously at the comedian's risqué jokes.

5 The schoolboy sniggered / cackled as the teacher sat down on the drawing pin he had placed on his chair.

Listening

You are going to hear two women talking about how they were dishonest in their youth.

1 🎧 **15.2** Listen to the recording once and decide which statement is true.

a They are both proud of what they did.

b Neither of them is proud of what she did.

c One of them is proud of what she did.

2 Before you listen again check that you know these American English words and expressions.

a bunch of money: a lot of money	cheater: a cheat
a stack of bills: a pile of bank notes	math: mathematics
a snap: easy	stuck: put

3 🎧 **15.2** Listen again and choose the best answer.

1 Speaker 1 was dishonest because
   a she was a bully.
   b she sympathized with someone.

2 Speaker 1
   a gave the money to the poor girl.
   b hid the money somewhere.

3 The rich girl
   a probably didn't know she had been robbed.
   b found the stolen money.

4 When speaker 2 was at High School
   a she was bad at all subjects.
   b she got poor grades for mathematics.

5 Speaker 2
   a planned in advance to cheat in the exam.
   b made up her mind to cheat during the exam.

Follow up: synonyms

4 **a** Match the highlighted words and phrases from the recordings with their synonyms.

1 ☐ *I felt so sorry for* that poor girl …
2 ☐ *I happened to be* by myself …
3 ☐ *Looking back* … I was really glad I did it.
4 ☐ *There's no way I'm going to* be able to…

a I'll never
b sympathized with
c by chance I was
d in retrospect

b Complete these sentences with an appropriate phrase from 4a in the appropriate form.

1 I suppose .... it was a silly thing to do.

2 I don't .... her at all. She brought it on herself.

3 I .... find this when I was clearing out the attic.

4 .... he'll get the job. He isn't qualified.

16

Language focus

Habits and predictable behaviour SB p.119

1 Complete this text with an appropriate verb in an appropriate form, making any necessary changes to word order. Use *will* where possible.

If I stay up watching television until late, I *'ll find* ¹ it difficult to get to sleep when I eventually go to bed. If I can't sleep, I .... ² myself a sandwich or something.

No matter what time I go to bed I .... ³ (always) my alarm clock for 7 a.m. except for Sundays when I .... ⁴ in until about twelve.

I tend .... ⁵ to bed until I've seen the late evening news, so around ten thirty. But if I've had a hard day I sometimes turn in as early as nine o'clock so I .... ⁶ as much as ten hours' sleep on some occasions.

If I've had a really heavy lunch and especially if I've had a few glasses of wine too, I often .... ⁷ off in front of the television, which is a bit embarrassing.

I've got a lot on my mind at the moment so I .... ⁸ difficulty getting to sleep. I tend .... ⁹ awake for ages worrying about things.

The passive SB p.121

2 Rewrite these sentences using appropriate passive forms.

1 You have to see this application form to believe it. The applicant has filled it in in gold ink.

   ....
   in gold ink.

2 The board will probably announce the name of the new chair at the next board meeting.

   ....
   at the next board meeting.

3 This was not the first time they had turned down his application.

   ....

4 They have appointed no one to Mr. Jones's old post since they promoted him last month.

   ....

5 They are going to hold interviews next week.

   ....

6 We ask candidates to send in a hand-written letter of application to accompany their CV.

   ....
   a hand-written letter of application to accompany their CV.

7 The company will require successful applicants to start work immediately.

   ....
   to start work immediately.

8 I'm sure they wouldn't have turned John down just because he has a beard.

   ....
   just because he has a beard.

9 You couldn't expect anyone with a degree to be happy doing that kind of job.

   ....
   to be happy doing that kind of job.

10 You must either type or word process your application.

   ....

🎧 **16.1** Listen, check, and repeat.

3 Complete this magazine article by putting the verbs in brackets in an appropriate form, making any necessary changes to word order.

▶ Note some verbs will be in the active voice.

Bamboo
– world super-plant

If you look closely enough at a stalk of bamboo, you should be able to see it growing. That's because it is the fastest-growing living thing on earth. The record .... **1** (set) in Japan, where the country's most common species .... **2** (grow) 120 centimetres in 24 hours – a rate that's just perceptible by the human eye.

Bamboo is also an extremely versatile plant. It's the most useful and well-used plant in the world. A list, ... **3** (compile) in Japan in 1903, detailed more than a thousand uses for the giant grass.

Bamboo .... **4** (eat) since time immemorial. Its shoots .... **5** (cherish) for their crispness and subtle flavour. The plant .... **6** (use) as a remedy for asthma, kidney ailments, and fever.

The hollow stalk, or *culm*, of the bamboo is only useful after three to five years' growth when it .... **7** (cut down) and .... **8** (polish up). Although the plant grows to its full height within 90 days, at this stage the culm .... **9** (consist) mainly of water. If it were cut this young, it would shrink and crack as it dried.

This young bamboo cannot withstand any pressure – unlike the mature culms, which are surprisingly strong. In Asia the grass .... **10** (use) for centuries as a building material. It's long-lasting as well as strong. In Europe bamboo .... **11** (grow) for decorative purposes. But care needs .... **12** (take) when growing it as it can cause havoc. As the plant .... **13** (reproduce) by underground stems, it is undeterred by fences or hedges and many species will spring up through metal or even tarmac.

Susannah Ward, Focus magazine

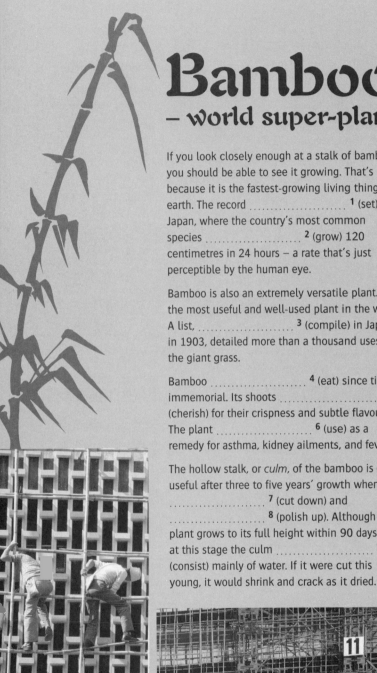

verb + object + *to* + infinitive SB p.123

4 Complete these sentences with an appropriate pronoun + infinitive.

1 Paula's teacher encouraged .... for university.

2 I absolutely forbid .... him again without my permission.

3 Will you speak to him? I can't get .... to a word I say.

4 She invited .... a seat but he said he preferred to stand.

5 Her father taught .... when she was five. She went on to represent her country in the 100 metres freestyle.

6 A driving licence permits .... a motorcycle as well as drive a car.

5 Rewrite the sentences using an appropriate verb from this list.

advise bear cause expect invite persuade prefer

1 'Why don't you both come round for a drink on Saturday?' Ailsa said.

Ailsa .... for a drink on Saturday.

2 'If I were you, I'd try going to bed at the same time each night,' the doctor said.

The doctor .... going to bed at the same time each night.

3 The car skidded on the ice.

The ice ....

4 I'll almost certainly be late.

Don't .... on time.

5 I hate you seeing me like this.

I .... me like this.

6 I'd rather you did your homework now.

I .... your homework now.

7 'All right, Jason, I'll go to the gym with you,' Patrick said.

Jason .... to the gym with him.

Other patterns

6 Choose the correct highlighted alternative in these sentences.

1 She insisted on me having / that I would have another slice of cake.

2 When I said I didn't feel well she suggested I went / me going to bed.

3 The current advertising campaign tries to discourage young people from smoking / to smoke.

4 Sunscreen should prevent you from getting / get burnt.

5 You can't make her to do / do something she doesn't want to.

6 I don't let my children stay / to stay up after nine on school nights.

7 I was made wear / to wear a uniform when I was at school.

8 Please allow me introduce / to introduce myself.

Vocabulary focus

Applying for a job SB p.123

1 a Complete this table.

verb	noun	noun (person)
	application	
X	....	candidate
	....	
employ		....
		....
graduate		
	interview	....
		....
	qualifications	X
refer		

b Check your answers then complete these sentences with an appropriate word from 1a.

1 The .... situation is such that .... have a great deal of choice when taking on new workers.

2 There have been over 500 .... for the job.

3 The panel will consist of three ....

4 Although you do not have to have a degree, preference will be given to ....

5 Please provide the names of two .... to support your application.

Vocabulary expansion

-ing adjectives

1.12 *soothing*   1.25 *relaxing*

1 a Before you read this magazine article, choose which answer you think is correct.

1 If you have problems sleeping the latest time you should have a coffee is about 2 p.m. / 6 p.m.

2 If you have difficulty getting to sleep you shouldn't do aerobic exercise in the evenings / just before you go to bed.

3 If you smoke, a cigarette in bed will / won't help you get to sleep.

4 Having a regular bedtime will / won't help you get a better night's sleep.

5 For a good night's sleep, your bedroom should be warm / cool.

6 Listening to the radio is a more / less effective way of relaxing than watching the TV.

b Read the article and check your answers.

2 a Match these *-ing* adjectives with the words they can collocate with.

appetizing   intoxicating   invigorating   refreshing
soothing   stimulating

1 .... music, voice, comments, ointment

2 .... food, smell (of something cooking)

3 .... drink, experience, effects (of drugs or alcohol)

4 .... shower, exercise, massage, run

5 .... conversation, ideas, lecture

6 .... change, shower, sleep, drink

b Complete these sentences with an appropriate *-ing* adjective from 2a.

1 .... liquor cannot be sold to persons under the age of eighteen.

2 We went for a brisk .... walk along the cliff path.

3 A .... breeze from the sea made the temperature more pleasant.

4 He woke up to the .... aroma of fresh coffee.

5 When I told Alan I had lost my job, he made some .... comments telling me that I would soon get another one.

6 We had a .... discussion on the subject of morality.

Trouble getting to sleep and don't want to resort to medication? Here are some tried and tested remedies.

■ Keep a regular sleep schedule. Go to bed and
5 get up at the same time every day. Stay in bed for 7–8 hours a night.

■ Steer clear of caffeine after early afternoon.
10 Try a herbal tea instead. Many, such as camomile, are soothing and have proven sedative qualities.

■ Don't smoke just before bedtime – nicotine is a
15 stimulant. Excessive alcohol consumption will not help you to sleep either – quite the
20 contrary.

■ Make sure your bedroom is cool, quiet, and dark.

■ A warm bath is relaxing
25 and will help to make you feel sleepy.

■ Don't watch T.V. in bed – the flickering screen stimulates rather then
30 relaxes the brain. Try listening to the radio with your eyes closed instead.

■ Aerobic exercise will help you sleep better, but not
35 immediately before bedtime.

■ Finally, if you feel sleepy during the day, have a short nap between noon
40 and 4 p.m., but not later than that or you'll find it impossible to get to sleep later on.

Sweet dreams!

dream and *sleep*: words and expressions

3 a Do you think these sentences are True or False?

1 ☐ If you sleep like a log, you have a good night's sleep.

2 ☐ If you dream up a plan, you think of it while you are in bed.

3 ☐ If somebody in a company is described as a sleeping partner, they are being criticized for not doing enough work.

4 ☐ If someone says 'Sweet dreams' to you, they are wishing you a good night's sleep.

5 ☐ If someone asks you if you'll sell them your car and you say you'll sleep on it, it means you don't want to decide there and then.

6 ☐ If you tell someone that you want to be a movie star and they say, 'Dream on!' they admire you for your ambitions.

7 ☐ You might daydream when you have a short sleep in the afternoon.

8 ☐ If someone sleeps in, they get up later than usual.

b Check your answers, then complete these sentences with an appropriate word or phrase from 3a in an appropriate form.

1 He spent the afternoon .... when he should have been working.

2 Many people .... on Sundays.

3 A Was the bed comfortable?

 B Yes, I ....

4 A Would you be interested in buying my car?

 B I'd like to but I'm not sure if I can afford it. Can I ....?

5 A I'm off to bed. Goodnight.

 B Night. ....

6 A If Brad Pitt asked me out ...

 B .... !

Listening

1 Before you listen to Jo talking about dreams, answer these questions about yourself.

1 Do you have a recurring dream?

2 What do you think causes it?

2 🎧 **16.2** Listen to the recording. How does Jo answer the questions in 1?

3 🎧 **16.2** Read the statements below. Then listen again and decide if they are True or False.

1 ☐ Jo has the dream when she's on holiday with her family.

2 ☐ In the dream, she finds it difficult to pack all her family's belongings.

3 ☐ In her dream, she always misses the plane.

4 ☐ She has not consulted a psychologist about her dream.

5 ☐ She has no idea what the dream means.

Follow up: idioms with *get*

It's to do with getting rid of things

4 Decide if the following sentences are True or False.

1 ☐ If somebody gets rid of their old clothes, they throw them away.

2 ☐ If somebody tells you to get a move on, they want you to move to another place.

3 ☐ If somebody gets on your nerves, they make you nervous.

4 ☐ If you get down to business, you set up in business.

5 ☐ If you get the hang of something, for example skiing, you manage to do it.

Language focus

Dependent prepositions SB p.127

1 Choose the correct highlighted alternative in these sentences.

1 I see you've finished that painting. Are you pleased about / with the way it's turned out?

2 Guy isn't at all pleased about / with the gallery's decision not to exhibit his work.

3 I'm angry about / with the amount of taxpayers' money that is spent on public works of art.

4 Justin is afraid for / of criticism, which is why he never puts his work on show.

5 I'm afraid for / of the future of the gallery. I'm concerned it might have to close.

6 We are grateful for / to the company for / to helping to finance the project.

7 Helen is angry about / with you for not inviting her to the opening.

8 I feel sorry about / for the people who have to look at that monstrosity every day.

9 A I like being an artist and I like being my own boss – responsible for / to no one but myself. What about you?

   B I'm the exact opposite. I work for a multinational and I'm responsible for / to the promotion of new products.

10 A Max should become a carpenter when he leaves school. He's good at / for / with his hands.

   B I think he should become a sculptor. He's good at / for / with creating things. He should go to Art School. It'd be good at / for / with him. He'd learn a lot.

🎧 **17.1** Listen, check, and repeat.

2 Complete these sentences with an appropriate verb from this list in the appropriate form, adding a suitable preposition.

accuse   aim   apply   congratulate   criticize   depend
object   resort

1 Nowadays many artists .... sponsorship from private companies or wealthy individuals.

2 The architect was .... designing a building which did not fit in with those around it.

3 The exhibition is .... young people and is designed with their interests in mind.

4 The resident .... the sculpture being placed in front of the building where he lived.

5 Up-and-coming artists can .... a grant to help them set themselves up in business.

6 The government was .... wasting public money on the work of art.

7 If the government doesn't increase the money they give to museums, they will have to .... charging an admission fee.

8 The judge .... him .... winning the prize.

Reference words and phrases SB p.129

3 Choose the best highlighted alternative in this text.

Pop Art is a movement in art. This / It ¹ is based on the imagery of pop culture and consumerism. These / Both ² had become integral features of American and to a lesser extent British society by the mid-1950s. Pop Art's main exponents were American and British artists. It / They ³ used advertisements, comic books, packaging, and images from T.V. and the cinema as sources of inspiration. Two of the most famous American exponents were Andy Warhol and Roy Lichtenstein. The former / This ⁴ achieved fame with his stencilled pictures of Campbell's soup cans. That / The latter ⁵ became known in the 1960s for paintings inspired by American comic strips of the 40s and 50s. Lichtenstein grew up with comics. These / Those ⁶ were the source of his inspiration.

4 a Complete this article with one of these words.

his   it (x2)   that   they   those   what   whose

ANTONY GORMLEY really does not have much to complain about over the reception for .... ¹ Angel of the North. Whatever the musings of the London critics – and most of .... ² who bothered to go and look were converted – the people who will have to live with the rust-coloured figure looming over their homes seem to have accepted the Angel as one of their own; a steel Geordie of fabulous size and strength but .... ³ wings arouse a twinge of pity. With the span, as we were repeatedly told, of a jumbo jet, ... ⁴ are both a marvel and a curse; like flight itself, liberating and yet containing the potential for inflicting great destruction. .... ⁵ has annoyed Gormley is to hear the Angel described as brash and meaningless. '............. ⁶ is extremely hurtful. The form is not invented. .... ⁷ is discovered. At the core of the Angel is half an hour of my life that was captured in plaster.' A key stage in the four-year evolution of the figure now overlooking the A1 near Gateshead was the 1:10 scale model Gormley made from a plaster mould of himself. .... ⁸ is how he works. Gormley believes it is 'silly' to try to invent natural bodies when he inhabits one of his own.

Extracted from an article by Stephen Goodwin first published in the *Independent Saturday Magazine* 28 February 1998

b Say what each of the reference words or phrases refers to.

1 *Antony Gormley's* .....   5 ....

2 ....   6 ....

3 ....   7 ....

4 ....   8 ....

Vocabulary focus

Male and female words SB p.131

1 Underline any sexist language in these sentences and replace it with an appropriate alternative.

1 The shirt is made of man-made fibres.
....

2 Barmaids and barmen are not generally well-paid.
....

3 The school has appointed a new headmaster. Mr Johns will take up his appointment in the new year.
....

4 I was stopped by two policemen, who insisted on breathalysing me. ....

5 The report says that the department is probably inefficient because it is undermanned.
....

6 The gas company said that they would send a man to investigate the leak immediately. ....

7 No man had ever walked in space before.
....

8 Experienced air-hostesses are required by an international airline. ....

9 Mankind is responsible for most of the ecological problems in the world today. ....

10 All members of staff and wives are invited to the annual summer ball. ....

Vocabulary expansion

1 Read this newspaper article and decide on the best title.

a What makes some women so special?

b Don't climb up there! It's dangerous!

c The trouble with women who do too much

INTREPID **WOMEN** have always existed. Their exploits may no longer cause scandal but they still run the male gauntlet of criticism and innuendo, writes Angela Lambert.

Remarkable women, women blessed with a combination
5 of physical stamina, psychological independence, and mental discipline, have always existed. They seem to crave feats of endurance or triumph to prove to the world, and themselves, that they are not like other women – and not like men either.

10 But if a strong physical and mental constitution is the prerequisite for the amazing exploits these women perform, the second has to be a supreme disregard for convention. Men who ride camels through the desert are unquestioned heroes for both sexes. Their female equivalents, however,
15 have to run the gauntlet of criticism and innuendo. The glib male view is that such women must either be freaks or embittered – disappointed in love.

One consequence of this antagonism is that remarkable women, having proved that they have powers of endurance
20 equal to those of remarkable men have as great, if not greater, a need to discover their innermost nature and being. Much of their own self-doubt has been programmed into them by men – and, it ought to be said,
by other women as well. Every mother
25 who tells her daughter, 'Don't climb up there, it's dangerous!' or 'Make sure your brother goes with you when you ride your bike,' introduces a fear of physical inferiority, as well as the notion –
30 probably true– that men prefer women to be weaker than themselves.

Extracted from an article by Angela Lambert first published in *The Independent* 1 July 1995

Criticism words

2 **a** Complete this text with an appropriate preposition.

> Women who do dangerous things are criticized .... **1** risking their lives when they have young children. The tabloid press really lay .... **2** them, accusing them of putting their own interests above those of their family. The press don't, however, find fault .... **3** men who do similar things. It seems to me that if you are going to have a go .... **4** a woman adventurer for being a bad mother, then it is only fair to bad-mouth men – most of whom are fathers – too.

b Cross out any adverbs and adjectives which do not collocate with the highlighted words below.

1 strongly / greatly criticize

2 fierce / hard / harsh / severe / constructive / heavy / strong / widespread criticism

3 be highly / sharply critical of somebody or something

c Complete these sentences with appropriate words or expressions from 2a and 2b.

1 I don't know why Emma doesn't just finish with her boyfriend. She spent the whole evening .... him.

2 The report was .... of the way the investigation had been handled.

3 Would you tell me what you think of this? It's my new novel. Any criticism, as long as it's ...., would be welcome.

4 The government's decision to raise the interest rate attracted ....

Idioms with *run*

> **1.2** *run the gauntlet*

3 Complete the idioms in these sentences with a word from this list.

course family form mill riot risk

1 A I see Brian's running true to ....

   B Yes, he always gets drunk at weddings.

2 Some people spend a fortune on cold remedies but I think it's better to take nothing and just let a cold run its ....

3 Their latest album is quite ordinary – very run-of-the- ....

4 If you cheat on your partner, you run the .... of ending your marriage.

5 Both her parents and her grandparents were musical. It runs in the ....

6 The children ran .... the moment the teacher left the room, throwing books and toppling over chairs.

Listening

You are going to hear Sean and Phiona talking about two pieces of public art.

1 🎧 **17.2** Listen to each recording once and answer these questions.

1 Which piece of art are they talking about?
2 Does the speaker like the piece?
3 What do the people who live there think about the piece?
  a They like it.
  b They don't like it.
  c We don't know how they feel about it.

2 🎧 **17.2** Listen to each recording again and decide whether these statements are True or False.

Recording 1

1 ☐ People have heard of Milton Keynes because it is a new town.
2 ☐ The residents dislike the piece because it is made of concrete.
3 ☐ Not many people have actually seen the work of art.
4 ☐ The piece looks life-like.

Recording 2

1 ☐ The work of art is in an old town near Bogotá.
2 ☐ The piece consists of a wall and several statues.
3 ☐ The piece contains bits of coloured glass.
4 ☐ People can't see the piece when they are sitting in the plaza.

Follow up: linking between words

> When we speak we sometimes run one word into the word which follows it.
>
> This happens when a word ending in a consonant is followed by a word beginning with a vowel.

3 a Look at these extracts from the recording and mark where you think there will be linking between words.

1 I'm living in a place called Milton Keynes at the moment …
2 … this is a …
3 … a town that is quite …
4 … for one of its particular works of public art …
5 … very few people have actually seen them …
6 … everybody's heard of them …
7 … How are the concrete cows?
8 … the residents of the town …
9 … a source of …
10 … of shame and embarrassment …

b 🎧 **17.3** Listen and see if you were right.

18

Language focus

Sentence structure SB p.135

1 Expand these notes into compound sentences. Join ideas with an appropriate conjunction from this list. Use each item once only.

~~and then~~   but   or   so   yet

1 People chosen Castaway 2000 project / sent to island of Taransay

People were chosen for the Castaway 2000 project ....
and then sent to the island of Taransay. ....

2 had to grow own food / starve if not

....

3 allowed keep farm animals like cows / had source of milk

....

4 didn't sleep ordinary houses / slept in special 'pods'

....

5 People found difficult experience / not missed it for the world

....

2 Rewrite the sentences below in one complex sentence using the words in bold.

1 We should deny criminals their moment of glory. We could reduce crime this way.

by

.... their moment of glory.

2 Some people are desperate for fame. These people will do anything to get it.

who

.... to get it.

3 We could refuse to use the names of criminals. Then they wouldn't become famous.

if

.... they wouldn't become famous.

4 A young man in ancient Greece burned down a temple. He hoped he would be remembered.

hoping

.... burned down a temple.

5 A criminal may achieve overnight fame. However, it doesn't last long.

although

...., it doesn't last long.

get SB p.137

3 Rewrite these sentences with *get* in an appropriate form.

1 You'd better go to the optician's. Your eyes need testing.

You'd better ....

2 All his windows were broken in the blast.

.... in the blast.

3 It would be terrifying to lose your way in the desert.

It would be terrifying .... in the desert.

4 His car was stolen and never recovered.

His car was stolen and he never

....

5 I won't be able to finish this work today.

I won't .... today.

6 Let's unpack these suitcases before we change our clothes.

Let's .... before we ....

🎧 **18.1** Listen, check, and repeat.

Phrasal verbs with *get* SB p.137

4 a Choose the correct highlighted particle(s) in these phrasal verbs.

1 I'm not sure how we'll get at / by now Joe's lost his job but I dare say we'll manage somehow.

2 Julia knows when her son has been getting out of / up to something he shouldn't because he doesn't look her in the eye.

3 I really don't want to go to my boss's wedding but I don't know how to get out of / by it.

4 I don't get by / on with my mother-in-law at all. I'm just not good enough for her precious son, it seems.

5 A I can't seem to get on / round to filling in my tax form.

   B I'm the same. It's so easy to find more important things to do, isn't it?

6 I hate my boss. She's always getting to / at me for no reason.

b Check your answers, then complete these sentences with an appropriate phrasal verb from 4a in the appropriate form.

1 Stop .... me! If you're not happy, do it yourself!

2 Neil is a very mischievous little boy. He's always .... something.

3 A How does Joachim always manage to .... the washing up?

   B He uses his charm on me and it works.

4 I've been meaning to clean out that cupboard for years but I'm not sure if I'll ever .... it.

5 Emma took a part-time job because they couldn't .... on her husband's salary.

6 A How do you manage to .... so well with Rebecca? She isn't the easiest of people to work with.

   B I just agree with everything she says.

Vocabulary focus

Fame SB p.134

1 Complete these sentences with an appropriate noun (or related noun or adjective) from this list.

celebrity   fame   glory   heroism   notoriety
renown   reputation   ~~villainy~~

1 Some of the James Bond *villains* are as well known as 007 himself – for example Odd Job in *Goldfinger*.

2 James Earl Ray achieved .... when he shot dead the black civil rights leader Martin Luther King in 1968.

3 The proud parents basked in the .... of their son's success.

4 Tom Hanks is an actor of international ....

5 The boy received a medal for his act of .... He had jumped into a river and saved his brother from drowning.

6 The awards ceremony was attended by a host of ....

7 Washington is .... for its museums and art galleries and, of course, the White House.

8 The actor has a .... for womanizing and drinking.

Vocabulary expansion

1 Read this extract from a novel and answer these questions.

   1 Where is the beach?

   2 Why do they want to find it?

'I know where the beach is,' I said.
Etienne raised his eyebrows.
'I've got a map.'
'A map of the beach?'

5 'The dead guy drew it for me. I've got it in my room.'
'A map,' said Etienne quietly. ' Can I see it? Would you mind?'
'Sure,' I said. 'Let's go.'

10 Etienne gazed at the map for five minutes without speaking. Then he said, 'Wait' and darted out of my room. I heard him rummaging around next door, then he came back holding a guidebook. 'There.' He

15 pointed to an open page. 'These are the islands in the map. A national marine park west of Ko Samui and Ko Pha-Ngan. Look. All the islands have protection. Tourists cannot visit, you see?'

20 I couldn't. The guidebook was written in French, but I nodded anyway.
Etienne picked up his guidebook and began a halting translation. 'The most adventurous travellers are exploring the islands beyond Ko

25 Samui to find … to find, ah, tranquility, and Ko Pha-Ngan is a favourite destination. But even Ko Pha-Ngan is … .' He paused. 'OK, Richard. This says travellers try new islands beyond Ko Pha-Ngan because Ko Pha-Ngan

30 is now the same as Ko Samui.'
'The same?'
'Spoiled. Too many tourists. But look, this book is three years old. Now maybe some travellers feel these islands are also spoiled.

35 So they find a completely new island, in the national park.'
'But they aren't allowed in the national park.'
Etienne raised his eyes to the ceiling. 'Exactly! This is why they go there. Because there will

40 be no other tourists.'
'The Thai authorities would just get rid of them.'
'Look how many islands are there. How could they be found? Maybe if they hear a

45 boat they can hide, and the only way to find them is if you know they are there – and we do. We have this.' He slid the map across the bed at me. 'You know, Richard, I think I want to find this beach.'

Alex Garland

Collocations: parts of the body

> **1.2** *Etienne raised his eyebrows*

2 a Match the idioms with the emotions they typically express.

   1 ☐ raise one's eyebrows

   2 ☐ shrug one's shoulders

   3 ☐ wrinkle (up) one's nose

   4 ☐ lick one's lips

   5 ☐ stamp one's foot

   6 ☐ drum one's fingers

   a show distaste, disgust

   b show surprise or disapproval

   c show annoyance

   d show impatience

   e show doubt, indifference

   f show eager anticipation for something enjoyable

b Check your answers then complete these sentences with an appropriate phrase from 2a in an appropriate form.

   1 Marie looked at the cheque and ………………………… at the thought of having so much money to spend.

   2 It's no good you …………………………. We're not getting a dog and that's that!

   3 Helen ………………………… on the table. She had been waiting twenty minutes for the waitress to bring her coffee. Was it ever going to arrive?

   4 'What do you fancy doing this evening, Angie?' Robert asked. Angie ………………………….'I don't mind. You decide.'

   5 Katy ………………………… at the news that Josie and Peter were having a baby. They had only been married a week.

   6 Angus ………………………… when the dish of snails was placed in front of him. No way would he be able to eat them.

Verbs: ways of looking for something

1.13 rummaging

3 a Read these verbs and their definitions.

go through:	examine something carefully in order to find something which is lost or deliberately hidden
ransack:	search thoroughly and roughly (causing untidiness and damage) usually with the intention of stealing something
rummage (about / around):	look for something among a lot of other things by moving them about with your hands
search:	look carefully in order to find something; examine a person in order to find something hidden
seek:	look for something you need, especially through an advertisement
scour:	search very carefully and thoroughly, looking for something important that is difficult to find

b Choose the best highlighted alternative in these sentences.

1 Police officers scoured / ransacked the area looking for the murder weapon.

2 The house had been rummaged / ransacked but nothing seemed to be missing.

3 Visitors to the prison are thoroughly searched / scoured .

4 I've rummaged about / been through every drawer in the house, but I can't find it anywhere.

5 24-year-old, new to area searches / seeks new friends. Box no 5234.

6 Natasha ransacked / rummaged about in her handbag for a good five minutes before finally producing the keys with a flourish.

Listening

You are going to hear Phiona talking about getting away from it all.

1 Before you listen, answer these questions about yourself.

1 Would you like to get away from it all?
2 What do you think you would miss about your life at the moment?
3 What would you least miss?

2 🎧 **18.2** Listen to the recording once. How does the speaker answer the questions in 1?

3 🎧 **18.2** Listen again and answer these questions.

1 Why would Phiona like to live on a yacht?
2 What would the main problem of living on a yacht be?
3 What would she miss about cafés?
4 What wouldn't she miss having to do every day?
5 What do people worry about?
6 What do we spend a large part of our lives doing?

4 Look at the tapescript on p.87 and find words or phrases with these meanings.

1 doing what you want to do ....
2 explain why you are doing something ....
3 sound of people talking quickly in a way that is difficult or impossible to understand ....
4 fierce and intense ....
5 become anxious ....

Follow up: *simple*

5 The speaker talks about *living a simple life*. The words *simple* and *simply* have several different meanings. See how many you know by answering these questions.

1 If a bedroom is simply furnished would it contain
   a cheap furniture?
   b a bed, wardrobe, chair and chest of drawers?

2 If you live a simple life would you
   a have very few possessions?
   b not go out a lot?

3 If a person were described as simple would they
   a take it as a compliment?
   b be insulted?

4 If you like simple food would you prefer
   a meat and potatoes?
   b roast duck in orange sauce?

Tapescripts

I think the person who in my life who who's em has influenced me in an extremely important way is em my great aunt – I call her Auntie Frances. She's my grandmother's sister and er she contracted multiple sclerosis when she was my age in fact 21 and er em I I've only know her obviously for my for my lifetime and that's sort of right towards the end of her life – she's 69 now em, in fact no, she's 79, 79 erm and erm the thing that that I find very important about her is that, well first of all she has outlived the average expectancy for someone with multiple sclerosis by about 30 years em which is absolutely incredible and and despite being in a lot of pain, despite not being able to eat, despite spending the last 50 years in residential care she er she still has an extremely on-the-ball em and sort of wicked sense of humour and er I think that's I find that every time I see her and I don't actually see her as often as I should. I always just find that absolutely incredible, she never seems miserable, she's always er extremely excited to have seen someone. People visit her regularly because she is er she is so kind of an inspiring person, and em she is never self-pitying, she is never, kind of, she never tries to draw attention to herself or her illness, em she's in and out of hospital all the time and er she just she she genuinely genuinely seems to enjoy life erm and just enjoy people around her and enjoy…

1.3

1   Katie's aunt's called Auntie Mary.
    No, she's called Auntie <u>Frances</u>.

2   Frances got multiple sclerosis when she was twenty-three.
    No, she got it when she was twenty-<u>one</u>.

3   She stays in a retirement home.
    No, she stays in a resi<u>den</u>tial home.

4   She's been there for the last fifteen years.
    No, she's been there for the last <u>fifty</u> years.

5   She's got a poor sense of humour.
    No, she's got a <u>wicked</u> sense of humour.

2.2

Part 1

When Anna had unpacked the case she had brought with her, had prepared and eaten her meal and given Griselda a chicken leg, she began to wonder if the owner of the cat she had run over would phone. The owner might feel, as people bereaved in great or small ways sometimes did feel, that nothing could bring back the dead. Discussion was useless and so, certainly, was recrimination. It had not, in fact, been her fault. She had been driving fast, but not illegally fast, and even if she had been driving at 30 miles an hour she doubted if she could have avoided the cat, which had streaked so swiftly out of the hedge.

It would be better to stop thinking about it. A night's sleep, a day at work, and the memory of it would recede. She had done all she could. She was very glad she had not just driven on as the next-door neighbour had seemed to advocate. It had been some consolation to know that the woman had so many cats, not just the one, so that perhaps losing one would be less of a blow.

Part 2

When she had washed the dishes and phoned her friend Kate, she wondered if Richard, the man who had taken her out three times and to whom she had given this number, would phone, and having decided he would not, she sat down beside Griselda, not with Griselda but on the same sofa as she was on, and watched television. It got to 10 p.m. and she thought it unlikely the cat woman – she had begun thinking of her as that – would phone now.

There was a phone extension in her parents' room but not in the spare room where she would be sleeping. It was nearly 11.30 p.m. and she was getting into bed when the phone rang. The chance of it being Richard, who was capable of phoning late, especially if he thought she was alone, made her go and answer it.

A voice that sounded strange, thin and cracked, said what sounded like, 'Maria Yackle.'

'Yes?' Anna said.

'This is Maria Yackle. It was my cat that you killed.'

Anna swallowed. 'Yes. I'm glad you found my note. I'm very sorry, I'm very sorry. It was an accident. The cat ran out in front of my car.'

'You were going too fast.'

It was a blunt statement, harshly made. Anna could not refute it. She said, 'I'm very sorry about your cat.'

'They don't go out much, they're happier indoors. It was a chance in a million. I should like to see you. I think you should make amends. It wouldn't be right for you just to get away with it.' Anna was very taken aback. Up till then the woman's remarks had seemed reasonable. She did not know what to say.

'I think you should compensate me, don't you? I loved her. I love all my cats. I expect you thought that because I had so many cats it wouldn't hurt me so much to lose one.'

That was so near what Anna had thought that she felt a kind of shock as if this Maria Yackle, or whatever she was called, had read her mind. 'I've told you I'm sorry. I am sorry, I was very upset, I hated it happening. I don't know what more I can say?'

'We must meet.'

'What would be the use of that?' Anna knew she sounded rude but she was shaken by the woman's tone, her blunt, direct sentences.

There was a break in the voice, something very like a sob. 'It would be of use to me.'

The phone went down. Anna could hardly believe it. She had heard it go down but still she said several times over, 'Hallo, Hallo?' and 'Are you still there?'

3.2

B   I don't actually em mind it when it rains, in fact, I quite like it sometimes, especially in erm in autumn if it rains and you're you're inside and you're in a nice warm house and you can hear the rain pattering down outside or see the raindrops running down the windows makes you feel quite quite cosy em but I mean I know a lot of people get very depressed with with the rain.

A   Yes, I do. And I think it's more the more the gloomy weather than the sort of dullness and darkness that you often get associated with rain em here that makes me depressed rather than the rain itself em 'cos I remember in Italy in the summer the it was very hot it had been hot for about well over a week with no rain at all and then suddenly one day it rained em and we all went outside and ran around in the rain 'cos it was cooling and refreshing but here when the weather's when it's when it's

overcast and dull I think that's what I find depressing and I think even then when whether you're inside or outside it's it's not much fun really…

B   … I think in some ways it depends, I mean there are certain kinds of rain that I don't like. I hate when it drizzles. It really irritates me when it drizzles. I, it just makes my hair frizzy, that's probably why, but I I like it when, I'd rather it was a real thunderstorm and a real torrential downpour and sort of got itself out of its system I mean in Europe it's nice em I lived in Barcelona for a while and it's nice there. In the summer it's quite common particularly in August the weather tends to break and you get these fantastic electric thunderstorms and they very conveniently take place at night so you can carry on during the day and then the temperature drops a bit em…

A   So it's clears the air?

B   Mm… well yes though sometimes it actually ends up being hotter or more humid after it's after it's actually rained but it's actually quite exciting to be in one of those electric storms. I can remember being at a pop concert once em and just just when the band came on stage em there was like a clap of thunder and a flash of lightning and a torrential downpour and there was nowhere to go and and everybody got absolutely soaked em and we were bone dry by the end of the concert so em that was quite exciting.

A   See you can't count on that in England though, can you? Here if it it can be thundery and stormy and it's not going to be suddenly beautiful and sunny afterwards. It's probably going to rain for another day or two em so I think I think when it happens suddenly and then stops it's not so bad but …

4.2

A   I do actually have one recollection. I don't think I am particularly em acutely aware of that that sort of thing extra-sensory stuff but I can remember once going on holiday to a little, it was actually a very old house and em and then there was this shrub. I know it sounds ridiculous but there was this shrub to the to the right of the front door and there was just this sense of I don't know that of something strange, malevolent, whatever lurking around this area and then upstairs I went with there were five of us altogether and once we were in this house at night we just we couldn't sleep upstairs we had to we all slept downstairs in the living room in a big in a you know, just together because we were frightened of being upstairs in the house there was just some, we all had this sense of something there of some some …

B   Presence

A   Yeah

B   Right. Frightening

A   Yeah…

5.2

Erm I think in scientific terms it's incredibly exciting erm and it seems to me to be in a way a logical and and inevitable extension of research into into the human genome and into working out exactly what makes life happen and what makes it tick erm so I don't think it could have been avoided and given that it's now happening erm I think people really need to get to grips with what the implications are and I don't think anybody has yet particularly. I know that there is talk of sort of religious leaders giving input to scientists on what they feel the moral implications of cloning are but that seems to me to be bringing together two worlds which at best have a very uneasy alliance and possibly really have nothing to do with each other at all erm so I would say, I wouldn't say I was personally particularly sort of either excited or worried by the possible implications of it erm it just seems to me to be another scientific development which will probably have some very undesirable side-effects as a lot of scientific developments have erm but which will also have some very desirable ones so I think that's probably just a natural sort of side-effect of what science does. But it isn't always a power for the good and it never will always be a power for the good.

6.2

Man 1 So if a child's identified as being particularly talented in some area, I don't know, musically or a potentially great athlete do you think they should receive special attention and training from an early age or do you think they should be just left alone to lead a normal childhood and hope that the cream will rise to the top, as it were?

Woman 1 It's difficult to know whether one would want to risk wasting that potential. On the other hand what's the most important is the child's happiness and normal development. I think it's very hard for a child not to be normal.

M1 Yeah.

Woman 2 I think the temptation must be great as well if you see your child with a very particular skill that that obviously they get pleasure from as well then I think the desire to to promote and encourage that must be great.

M1 All too often you see examples of children who have excelled ending up being very unhappy as adults 'cos having their childhood taken away from them.

W1 Yes, certainly.

W 2 And you could argue that behind every successful child is a pushy parent.

W1 Yes.

Man 2 It's a very new phenomena though, a lot of in the past people would move into an area of the arts or or sports at a later at a later stage in their lives and it was the ones that had that natural ability that were born with it that would then rise to the top but there were still at that stage a lot of people who weren't naturally athletic I guess or not naturally that much better than everyone else but because they'd just chosen to spend more time doing it excelled but now people are on the lookout so much for any natural ability which is which is which they are born with that they are all being snapped up and directed into specific areas and I think there is a bit of a danger there because a well-rounded personality and a life is becoming harder and harder to achieve.

W1 And the idea of a child having to be terribly competitive at a young age I think is very unhealthy.

All Umm.

W1 A child needs a childhood and being competitive takes away your childhood and then you have to think what's actually the

most important erm so it's a very difficult dilemma, I think.

W2 It is, because you could also argue that if somebody does have a tremendous gift say a wonderful musical gift that is going to give pleasure to hundreds, thousands of people, millions of people isn't there perhaps isn't that perhaps almost as if that that gift has come from somewhere and we could all argue that that's hereditary or you know you often hear people with a particular talent say that they feel that God has given them that, that they have this God-given gift and that perhaps in some way they often feel that it's almost their duty to nurture it and to share it so there is also that to be argued I suppose that if you do have something special that it's almost like part of that gift is to to is to share it with others.

7.2

Woman 1 Have you guys ever had déjà-vu before?

Woman 2 Oh, yeah, most definitely.

Man Sure.

Woman 3 Me too. Me too. Actually quite a number of times.

W2 Really?

W3 I've had it happen yeah.

W1 They say I've actually read somewhere that they think that you actually dreamt something and then when it happens in your life it's like you're re-living it for the second time.

M Really?

W1 that it really was more of a premonition … that you dreamt it before it happened.

W2 Really? I've also heard that it's your mind thinking ahead to what's going to happen and then when it happens you're like, 'Oh that's déjà-vu,' but I don't believe that. I go for more the maybe you dreamt it before or I mean I also believe in past lives so…

W1 Mm

M But if you dreamt it that's very intriguing because that would mean that that's premonition.

W1 Exactly. Premonition.

W2 Right.

M That's that's pretty amazing too.

W2 I definitely believe in premonition.

8.2

C Not being a parent myself I can perhaps only speak from my experience as a child and and programmes I've seen and what I've read about it. It seems to me that young children anyway particularly em need some sort of parental control because they need to know what the boundaries are of what they can and can't do and if they don't have those boundaries they just seem to go a bit crazy em I think those boundaries give them security and make them feel loved.

A Did you have boundaries like that when you were a child?

C Em yes I think I probably had too many boundaries em and I didn't feel secure. I'm not really I don't think it was because of that because there were lots of rules and regulations and things I knew I should and shouldn't do but I think although there's lots of

things I disagreed with em looking back on on my parent, the way my parents controlled me there were lots of things I couldn't do em which seemed a bit ridiculous and and seemed to be based on my parents not trusting me to behave in an appropriate way.

A Yeah

C Em because they assumed I would do something when In fact it never had crossed my mind to do that

A Yeah

C And and and that doesn't really help the relationship between you and your parents em

A Yes I think that's true of me as well. There were loads and loads of regulations and rules and I did feel secure and I did have a happy childhood but I think it made me as a parent it made me em realize that you didn't need quite as many rules and regulations as that so I think I was I certainly gave my children more freedom than I had and sometimes it's worked …

C Do you think it's important that parents are strict with em with people when they're when they're young?

L Em

C Or when they're teenagers even?

L I think it's important that there are certain rules set out and that the child or the teenager knows the boundaries em but there's a difference between setting out rules and being strict.

C So what boundaries would you say that it's necessary for parents to set?

L Em well children for example have to learn social behaviour and stuff when they're em when they're young so they need to know need to learn those rules like how to act in public how to behave around other people how to treat other people so rules like that are important.

C But you think that's different from being strict?

L Em strict is probably when you take it a little bit too far and maybe try and run the child's life or don't let the child make their own mistakes and learn from them but it's important to give them a bit of guidance in terms of rules.

C Do you think when you have children of your own will you treat them in the same way as your parents did or will you treat them in a different way?

L Em I'd say pretty much in the same way.

C So you think that they that they were strict enough but without being too strict?

L Yeah, definitely I mean there wasn't it's not as if I was made to stay in or anything if there was something I wanted to do quite often I was allowed to do it but then things again like homework and em other other things always got in the way every now and then but when you look back I guess they were for your own good that you actually did follow those rules so sometimes it's important to have rules.

9.2

Music is also really important to me. It's er as Jen said it's sort of it's a drug it's mood-altering. I love to drive and and listen to Baroque music, Vivaldi, and it's sort of it's sort of like supplying an orchestral score to your life. I remember when I got my very first Walkman um I had on the overture from from some Broadway show and I'd never had a Walkman before and all of a sudden I had the er the earphones and the sound was amazing it was so full I thought everybody else in

Bloomingdale's was hearing it too and I was on the escalator and just as the music is swelling I'm sort of rising to the top of the escalator and I thought, 'This is great! I have a musical score to my life now! I love movies so now here I have background music for my life!' Em also as Mara was saying it's it's cathartic, if you're really really happy or angry or depressed and you find a lyric that just matches it you can sort of get those feelings out through the music, which is a healthy way to deal with it I suppose, there are lots of worse ways to deal with it em but it's you know sort you know have a drink and put on Sinatra and there's there's no better therapy when you're really depressed or you're heart-broken and it it helps get you over it and em it has a major effect on me I can cheer myself up or or calm myself down or or like you said during a workout er pump myself up.

10.2

I'll never forget seeing the sunrise over Macchu Pichu in Peru the em ancient sacred site of the Incas. I don't think everybody's quite 100% sure what it is, what you'd call, whether you'd call it a temple or a city or whatever but em we'd em been walking for three days and the morning of the fourth day we got up incredibly early about quarter to four in the morning or something so we could get to the top of this mountain to be able to look down into the valley um to see Macchu Pichu at sunrise. The problem was of course that everybody else who was around – it was high season at the time, it was August – em everybody else had the same idea that everybody wanted to get to this site first, so at four o'clock in the morning on what should be this deserted mountain pass there were hundreds if not thousands of people pushing and shoving and walking along as fast as they could, some of them running, all with their rucksacks and their cameras and their camcorders trying to get trying to be the first to get to this spot so they could set up and get the best pictures. As it started to get lighter everybody was panicking that they were going to miss this great experience and got more and more frantic and more desperate, and people were elbowing other people out of the way and em it really wasn't very pleasant at all. We finally arrived at the at the spot we were supposed to be, 'The Sun Gate', which is where the best views of the valley were to be were to be seen, and the atmosphere out there I thought was horrible. Everybody was setting up their cameras, pushing people out of the way, em queuing basically, and it really wasn't what we'd walked four days and travelled thousands of miles to see, so we moved a little bit further down the mountain. We thought, you know, this is this is where everybody else is gonna be. Let's go and have a little bit of peace and em try and experience and appreciate this properly, and about half a mile walk down the mountain we found this other little ruin, which was deserted, and we sat in there and we had almost perfect silence except for the sounds of a few hummingbirds around this ruin and looked down and saw the valley suddenly being filled with lights, going from being a cold dark stony place and being touched by the sunlight, and everything started to turn to different colours of greens and the sky turned from grey to blue and the whole thing was just fantastic and breathtaking.

11.2

One of my earliest memories is erm I seem to remember it being a very hot day and my mum had plonked me in the garden on a a rug erm and my brother was playing in a in a in a little paddling pool erm to the left of me and I was I was trying to make my way to the paddling pool I was I was crawling along the erm along the grass and and I finally made it there and I just sort of I just sort of keeled over erm against the edge of the little paddling pool thing and of course when you do that all the water starts gushing out and erm and that's what happened and I can just remember this water this not very I think it was quite cold actually the water it just sort of drenching me erm and going all over my face and I just can remember screaming and crying and gurgling it was a mixture of pleasure and and and discomfort and surprise.

12.2

Man 1 I had one, a teddy bear named Brownie.
Woman 1 Oh, Brownie.
M1 And I got mad at my mother for something and with children's logic I took Brownie and defiantly threw him in the waste basket like 'There that'll fix you!' No I was I was holding him over the wastebasket threatening and my mother said, 'If Brownie goes in the waste basket he's not coming out.'
W1 Ooh!
M1 And I thought well 'Up yours lady!' and I threw him in the wastebasket.
W1 Ooh!
M1 That was it.
W1 Oh!
M1 And then my dad came over and said 'Why are you throwing Brownie away?' and I thought, 'Cos I cut off my nose to spite my face.'
W1 Ooh, Brownie!
Woman 2 Well I also used to collect rocks as a kid
Man 2 How exciting
W1 Rocks?
W2 Yes, rocks.
W1 Rocks like from outside rocks?
W2 Yes, rocks (laughter)
W1 That's weird
M2 Were some of them actually concrete?
M1 Did you name them? (laughter)
W2 Well I don't know. I guess it was my way like whenever anybody in my family would travel somewhere I'd ask them to bring me back a rock.
W1 Oh, that's sweet.
W2 So you know I'd have rocks from Hawaii (giggles) and rocks from California …
M1 Do you still have them?
W2 I – you know what? – they probably are still up in my mother's attic somewhere I really think…
M1 You could tell her relatives in airports. They couldn't lift their suitcases! (laughter)
W1 Did you label them? How did you know which rock was from which place?
W2 I don't even think I labelled them. I just sort of knew you know.
M1 Someday you'll have one heck of a rock garden!
M2 I was really into magic and I still am.
W2 Oh magic.
M2 You guys don't know that because I don't like to bore my friends with it.
M1 Thank you. We appreciate that.
W2 I've seen some of your tricks actually.
M2 Well (laughter) It was almost more of a just something for me to focus on because I loved practising more than performing and when no-one was home I would lay them all out on the coffee table and I would save money from doing odd jobs and cutting grass and I'd order tricks by mail order.
W2 Oh how fun.
M2 And sometimes I'd get my folks to take me downtown to to Al's Magic Shop and I'd spend a few bucks on tricks and er but I usually wouldn't get the courage to show them to many of my friends because then they'd challenge you, 'Oh, I know how you did it!'
M1 Yeah, 'I saw your hand move'.
M2 Yeah, or you feel like a heel if they say, 'How did you do that?' and you don't tell them. And of course that's the magic, magician's code.
M1 Magician's code.
M2 Never tell.
W2 You're not supposed to tell.
M1 Hide behind that.
M2 But you feel like you want to buy their favour and say, 'OK. I'll show you how I did it'. (laughter)

13.2

B Well look I mean I I just think it's a bit unfair because you know you say that this doesn't get done and you know you kind of imply that I'm the one that should do it but there's there's so much that isn't made clear to me.
W But Bill, aren't you aware that everyone else is in the same position as you? And I feel I get more commitment from other people.
B Well, yeah I mean well you know yeah I am committed but I mean for instance if if things come up on on the computer screen and they have a Post-it you mean it's never clear to me if I'm supposed to respond to it or if somebody else is. I mean I mean …
W Bill, it really rather sounds to me like a case of passing the buck. I'm sorry but if other people are coping with this situation I don't see why it's so difficult for you. And if you do have a problem then talk to somebody about it. Don't let it go and then we discover too late that things haven't been done.
B Well I mean it's not that it's a problem it's just that they're very vague areas and I I mean if I know if I'm supposed to do something that if that job falls within the jurisdiction of my responsibilities fine but there are times when I've asked people I should do it or if I should do something or if I shouldn't and it's never clear. I mean it's almost as if you know things things sort of get done and when they don't it just seems that it always you know ends up being my fault …
W Oh, I see. This is really the heart of the matter – that you feel that we're always blaming you.
B No it's not that but well I don't know really. I mean the thing is I can understand that you're saying that I lack commitment if I don't do things. It seems that I came here to do one thing and I'm asked so many times to do things that seem to fall outside…
W But Bill that's all …

14.2

If I really had a choice then I'd definitely change em and I think there are two possibilities, two things I really would like to do and which I've always wanted to do. One is to be a surgeon and another is to be a radio, well, electronics engineer either in computers or telecommunications. Surgery because engineering has always intrigued me the way things are built and the way things work er machines, I love machines, I love tinkering with machines and in a way the human body is is something like that. You've got all the various systems in the body and you've got all the various things like the bones and the various organs and it would be fascinating I think trying to repair this system. Really what I would most enjoy most of all to be an orthopaedic surgeon or a heart surgeon em I could never be an eye surgeon 'cos that would just 'cos eyes are just well disgusting eyes are just they're all squishy and squashy and unpleasant and brain surgery, I don't think I could ever do because I don't think I could be delicate enough to do that.

The difficulty I suppose the drawback if there is a drawback of course to be a surgeon is first of all the training, which is both expensive and em and very long what six, seven, eight years? And I'm not sure that I would have the determination or the discipline to do all that. There is of course the responsibility er because clearly you can't afford to make mistakes because people's lives are in your hands and I think I think I would be a little bit afraid of that. I think I would be able to cope with it but I think I would always be slightly worried of making mistakes.

15.2

Speaker 1

I was at camp and there was this girl who was extremely wealthy in my cabin and she used to constantly tease and make fun of this other girl in my cabin who was very poor and would literally just ridicule her about not having money and not having nice clothes and just I felt so sorry for that poor girl and that the rich girl was was very much of a bully and one day I came into the cabin and I happened to be by myself and I saw on the rich girl's bureau she had a bunch of money stacked there and I don't know what what came over me but I took $20 off of her stack of bills and stuck it in the poor girl's pillowcase (laughter). It was my own little Robin Hood fantasy I don't know what I was doing but I gave the poor girl the $20 I put it in her pillowcase and looking back I mean I felt really powerful at the time and I was really glad I did it I don't even think the rich girl ever noticed that it was missing 'cos she had so much money and looking back I think it was probably a pretty foolish thing to do because the $20 probably ended up in a laundry machine and the poor girl probably never even found it.

Speaker 2

Well I was a cheater. I'm not a cheater any more but I was a cheater in High School in em algebra. I was absolutely terrible at math had always been terrible at math used to get straight As and Cs in math and er I had entered this algebra class and I knew I just was like there's no way I'm going to be able to pass this this class so I befriended one of the smartest people in the class who for them algebra was just a snap and I remember one time we had this exam. I don't remember if it was a mid-term exam but basically, I still can't believe I did this and and I feel terrible about it, but when the teacher turned her back I handed my exam to this smart person in front of me. She filled out my whole exam and then handed it back to me and I turned it in. And I think I got

like a 90 per cent on it or something so I I actually yeah I passed the class but I passed the class because I cheated and er I can't say I feel very good about that. I actually feel pretty guilty about it but er you know I guess I did what I had to do em and I still can't do algebra to this day because of that.

16.2

I often have a very disturbing dream, I dream that I'm away on holiday with my family and then suddenly I'm told that it's time to leave and go to the airport to get the aeroplane home again but I haven't actually packed any of my things to go and I've only got a few minutes to actually get everything packed into my suitcases and get my luggage together to leave to get on the aeroplane but usually in my dream I've got all members of my family with them they've got lots of their toys, books, shoes, so I've got far too much to manage to stuff into the suitcase so I'm desperately trying to get everything packed away and in the suitcases to get back to the airport but I always wake up before I actually have to get on the plane.

I mean, it's a recurring dream, it's not connected to holidays at all, it's usually I think connected to times of stress, when I feel under pressure, probably sometimes when I've got changes going on in my life because I'm always, I'm unable to pack everything that I want to take with me so I'm having to make decisions about what I leave and what I take, which of the children's toys I get rid of and which I'm able to carry with me, or which of my clothes and shoes I'm able to, so I think maybe subconsciously and psychologically it's to do with sort of getting rid of things old and starting things new, perhaps it's something, but I've never spoken to a psychologist or I've never had anybody try and interpret that dream but that's my conclusion really of what I think it's about.

17.2

Speaker 1

I'm living in a place called Milton Keynes at the moment and this is a town that is quite famous, infamous really, for one of its particular works of public art, which is the concrete cows um. These exist by their reputation really in most people's minds I think em for because very few very few people have actually seen them but everybody's heard of them. People say. 'Ah, you're from Milton Keynes. How are the concrete cows?' Em I think for that reason the residents of the town feel they are a source of of shame and embarrassment rather than any source of civic pride or anything like that because to the world outside they've come to symbolize the city and its lack of lack of life lack of soul 'cos it is very concrete and em all very synthetic and people just think that it's, 'Even the even the cows are made of concrete. They haven't even got real live cows'. Um the piece in itself is quite quite nice. It's, very few people see it because it's just off a main road round the north of the town and in a field next to the road there are five or six cows more or less life-size, possibly a bit smaller, and em very realistic. I think when you're certainly when you're driving and you see them from a distance …

Speaker 2

I spent some time in Bogotá in Colombia and around the centre of the city – the old city – there is an area called the Candelaria em it's near the university and it's an old town, an amazing place, sort of old buildings and cobbled streets and er lots of little narrow winding streets em and it's great. There's a sort of mountain up behind it that you can see from there. It's em quite a run-down area em but it's got a lot of old character, quite historic. And there in the middle of it there's a sort

of sort of open space, a kind of plaza and there's em a little sort of art installation em it's kind of walls like curved walls em they're white and they've got these figures these human figures these statues – life-size – sitting like they're sitting in the windows on the first floor em one of them's wearing a top hat and sitting with a cane and and sort of sitting like he's just sitting in a window but he's – it's not really a wall going to anywhere, it's just a wall, em There's one that's dressed as a clown where he's sort of holding an umbrella open, like he's using it to balance em and I was there on a really sunny day and er there was people sort of sitting around in this plaza and this art was behind them and through the windows you could see the blue sky behind it em and the white against the blue was just a really nice contrast. It just looked like a painting. There was a sort of building or something behind that had coloured bits in the walls and it just there was this blue sky and these white art things and this coloured glass and it just it just looked really really good and er it seems to be quite a focal point of that area that you know just normal people, everyday lives and they're sort of living out their dramas and there's this art as their background it just looks really nice just the idea that 'cos Bogotá is really high up in the Andes and em there you are all the way up, high in the mountains, in the sunshine and there's this there's this art in a city and it's just really nice.

18.2

…so I think I would like to get away from it all and live a simple life. I don't know if I'll ever be able to afford to buy a yacht but I would like to and I think that would be a really nice way to live. I think it would be it would be a good way of sort of yeah spending time your own time doing your own thing em not having to sort of justify every minute of your day the way you do in a city em. What would I miss about that sort of life getting away from it all? I think I would miss the cinema, I would miss newspapers. I think I would miss spontaneity. I think if you're if you're living a life like that and you want to do something you really have to plan it. You have to work out when you're going to be in, in this case you have to work out when you're going to be in port, and if you're going to meet people, you have to work it out ages in advance. I think in a city one of the things that that's really great is if it's a sunny day you can go for a drink after work and not really have to plan it except beyond you know just just going off to the pub or maybe booking a table in a restaurant or something em so that spontaneity.

The other thing I think you might miss is you might miss, I might miss the idea of sort of going into a café and that sort of babble of voices in a café I think there's something very, there's a lot of energy and that there's a lot in that that would be really good. But you know I think yeah what I wouldn't miss would be the pace of a city, the sort of cut-throat ambitious, the survival of the fittest thing that, having to justify every minute of every day either to yourself or to an employer or you know go to work, go to the gym, go home, go to sleep, get up, in time for work de de de.

That you know people getting het up about stuff that just doesn't matter at all the you know people worrying about sort of small urban problems that really don't make any difference to the world and sort of crowded urban transport and traffic jams and sitting for hours and hours every day and if you add up the number of hours you spend in traffic I mean it's so long, such a vast proportion of your life spent sitting there just getting more and more frustrated and listening to stuff on the radio that really just doesn't matter so, yes a simple life would be nice.

Answer key

Unit 1

Language focus

1 1 In particular; eventually
2 Incidentally
3 to be honest; At first
4 Even so
5 To start with
6 To sum up

2 1 Foolishly
2 In retrospect
3 Apparently
4 understandably
5 A up to a point
B Personally
6 seriously
7 By the way

3 1 Neither
2 either
3 both
4 both
5 all
6 Neither
7 none
8 either
9 all
10 all

4 1 Alex can neither cook nor sew.
2 Tim, Bobby, and Lily all / They all / All of them like Italian food.
3 Quentin is both selfish and bad-tempered.
4 None of us like / likes ironing.
5 Both Bethany and Grace can speak a little German. Bethany and Grace can both speak a little German.

Vocabulary focus

1a

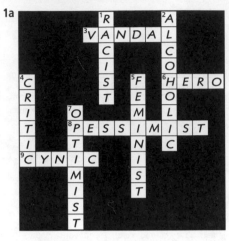

1b 2 alcoholism
3 vandalism
4 criticism
5 feminism
6 heroism
7 optimism
8 pessimism
9 cynicism

1c 1 cynic
2 vandals
3 optimists
4 feminist
5 heroism
6 criticism

2 1 couch
2 pain
3 bag
4 waste
5 loose
6 bright
7 lost
8 cool

Vocabulary expansion

1 1 False
2 True

2a *indelible*: mark; impression
(in)edible: food
inimitable: manner; style
(ir)responsible: behaviour; decision; manner
irreversible: breakdown; damage; decision
irrevocable: decision
marketable: goods; product; style
objectionable: behaviour; manner

2b 1 behaviour … objectionable
2 marketable products
3 irreversible damage
4 food … edible
5 decision … irreversible / irrevocable
6 inimitable manner / style

3 1 excruciatingly
2 positively
3 fiercely
4 worryingly
5 internationally

Listening

1 b

2 1 d
2 a
3 b
4 c

3 1 False. She got multiple sclerosis when she was in her early-twenties.
2 True
3 True
4 True
5 False. She *never* complains about being ill.

4a She's sixty-nine now em in fact <u>no</u>, she's <u>seventy</u>-nine, <u>seventy</u>-nine.

4b 2 <u>No</u>, she got it when she was twenty-<u>one</u>.
3 <u>No</u>, she stays in a <u>resi</u>dential home.
4 <u>No</u>, she's been there for the last <u>fifty</u> years.
5 <u>No</u>, she's got a <u>wick</u>ed sense of humour.

Unit 2

Language focus

1 1 ✔
2 ~~had been involved~~ / are involved
3 ~~am still working~~ / was / were still working
4 ~~would lend~~ / will lend
5 ~~won't be~~ / wouldn't be
6 ✔

2 2 but for the expense / but for the fact that it's so expensive
3 As long as you've got a modern phone / As long as you haven't got an old-fashioned phone
4 provided that they aren't / they're not over-used
5 Supposing you didn't have one

3
1. ~~didn't know~~ / ~~hadn't known~~
2. would … promise
3. would have been able
4. would be sitting
5. don't have / haven't got
6. would do
7. are
8. make / made / have made

4
1. were
2. would tear up
3. had gone
4. hadn't been delayed
5. would have been
6. moved
7. dug / would dig

5
2. would mind
3. did like
4. is / was ill
5. does love

6
1. Deirdre is a lovely girl.
2. Kieran said you weren't interested.
3. I'll definitely be there.
4. To my way of thinking, the book was too long. / The book was too long, to my way of thinking.
5. Ferraris are very nice to drive.
6. I'm really fed up with your attitude.

Vocabulary focus

1a
1. my day
2. do
3. a good turn
4. the most of
5. good
6. very well for himself
7. a mountain out of a molehill
8. a night of it

1b
1. make a mountain out of a molehill
2. make a night of it
3. do a good turn
4. do (someone) good
5. do very well for oneself
6. make the most of
7. make one's day
8. make do

Vocabulary expansion

2a

	Formal		Informal
2	the task in hand	6	come across
3	cause offence or confusion	7	get around
		8	popped up
4	pertinent to	9	kid

2b
1. kidding
2. overcome
3. properly
4. pertinent
5. pops up

Listening

1 b

2 See tapescript

3
1. False. They had been out together three times.
2. True
3. True
4. False. Maria Yackle put the phone down.

4
1. d
2. e
3. a
4. b
5. c

5
2. be taken aback
3. blow
4. consolation

Unit 3

Language focus

1
1. spoke
2. had studied
3. weren't
4. hadn't left
5. didn't have

2
2. could go
3. hadn't said / hadn't promised
4. could see / could meet
5. had brought / had
6. were; earned / had / made; lived / were living
7. had had / had been given; would stop / wouldn't keep

3
1. ~~had~~ / had had
2. ~~wouldn't be~~ / wasn't / weren't
3. ~~can~~ / could
4. ✔
5. ~~will~~ / would
6. ✔

4
1. Unfortunately, there is no way
2. a pity I didn't have
3. a shame we can't
4. If only … could be
5. would be (really) grateful if you didn't preserve
6. (really) hope people are never
7. sometimes sorry (that) the telephone was

5
1. B would / ~~could / might~~; would / ~~could / might~~
2. A would / ~~could / might~~
   B would / ~~could / might~~
3. B ~~would~~ / could / might
   A ~~would~~ / could / ~~might~~
   B would / ~~could / might~~
4. B ~~would / could~~ / might
5. B would / ~~could / might~~

6
1. would consist (*would* is more likely because of *claimed* but *could* is also possible)
2. would be
3. would be
4. would … change
5. would outweigh
6. could suffer / be suffering

Vocabulary focus

1a *active* interest
cultural differences; interest
dominant position
isolated incident; position
local differences; disasters; interest; position; response
natural differences; disasters; interest; position; response
negative outlook; position; response
positive outlook; position; response

1b
2. active interest
3. cultural differences
4. positive response
5. negative outlook
6. isolated incident
7. local interest
8. dominant position

Vocabulary expansion

1 1 False. It consists of water and a speck of dirt.
2 True
3 False. Only 3 %.
4 True

2 small: microscopic; minute; tiny
large: enormous; gigantic; huge; massive

3a 2 f
3 a
4 h
5 c
6 e
7 d
8 g

3b 1 a drop of rain
2 ray of sunshine
3 rumble of thunder
4 a speck of dirt
5 flakes of snow

4a 1 wet
2 hot
3 dry
4 hot
5 wet
6 cold
7 hot
8 cold

4b 1 dripping
2 soaking
3 scalding
4 boiling
5 piping
6 freezing
7 bitterly

Listening

1

	Beverley	Anthony
rain in autumn	a	c (but we suppose he doesn't)
gloomy weather	c	b
drizzle	b	c
thunderstorms	a	c

2 1 inside; cosy
2 dullness; darkness
3 cooling; refreshing
4 drizzle; her hair frizzy
5 hotter; more humid
6 got absolutely soaked

3 I don't actually em <u>mind</u> it when it <u>rains</u>, in fact, I quite <u>like</u> it <u>sometimes</u>, es<u>pe</u>cially in em in <u>autumn</u> if it <u>rains</u> and you're you're in<u>side</u> and you're in a nice <u>warm</u> <u>house</u> and you can hear the rain <u>pattering</u> down out<u>side</u> or see the raindrops <u>running</u> down the <u>windows</u> makes you feel quite quite <u>cosy</u> em but I mean I know a lot of people get <u>very</u> de<u>pressed</u> with with the <u>rain</u>.

Unit 4

Language focus

1a 1 knew
2 had caught
3 learnt
4 had pushed
5 had receded
6 happened
7 skidded
8 went
9 saw
10 turned over
11 fell

1b 1 had wondered
2 wasn't hearing
3 had begun
4 had struggled
5 began

1c 1 had heard
2 (had) called
3 arrived
4 had managed
5 was bleeding

2 1 had been stung
2 ✔
3 decided
4 ✔
5 didn't need
6 arrived
7 knew
8 ✔
9 called out

10 ✔
11 ✔
12 was wearing

3 1 stealing
2 on Mandy coming
3 to help
4 not to take
5 that she would be able
6 having
7 to give

4 2 decided to have the fish.
3 begged Geri to go out with him.
4 advised Roger not to buy a new car until prices dropped.
5 asked Rosa to repeat what she had said.
6 told me not to worry / and that it would be / was going to be all right.
7 forbade me to use the office phone for personal calls.
8 didn't think I would like / was going to like what she was going to suggest.

Vocabulary focus

1a

verb	adjective (to describe the effect of something)	adjective (to describe how you feel)	abstract noun
anger	X	angry	anger
annoy	annoying	annoyed	annoyance
irritate	irritating	irritated	irritation
frustrate	frustrating	frustrated	frustration
X	X	furious	fury

1b 1 furious
2 anger
3 annoying / irritating
4 frustrated
5 annoyance / irritation

2 1 the music
2 a mile
3 the deadline
4 the bush
5 the rush
6 facts
7 his match
8 a business

Vocabulary expansion

1b Four: the M3, the A30, the A322, and the A3.

2a 2 lane
3 trunk road
4 central reservation
5 carriageway
6 tailbacks

2b 1 lanes; lane
2 carriageway
3 tailback
4 junction
5 central reservation

3a 1 b
2 c
3 a

3b 1 suffering
2 were clogged
3 trigger

Listening

1 c

2 1 True
2 False
3 True
4 False
5 False

3 1 c
2 d
3 b
4 a

4a 1 presence
2 lurking
3 recollection
4 malevolent

4b 1 lurking suspiciously / in the shadows
2 constant presence
3 malevolent look / smile
4 vague recollection

Language focus

1a Students' own answers

1b 1 could
2 (would) suggest
3 would advise
4 What
5 ought to / should
6 not / doesn't she / he

1c 1 c
2 f
3 a
4 d
5 e
6 b

2 1 my view they should allow
2 completely disagree / disagree completely
3 not simply / don't you simply ask your boss
4 is my considered opinion that
5 can't / couldn't (possibly) go along

3 1 Hardly had the plane taken off when …
2 ✔
3 Not only was the man drunk, he was aggressive too.
4 Not once did the flight attendants lose their temper with the passenger.
5 ✔
6 Not since my first flight has anything so interesting happened.
7 At no time did the situation get out of control.
8 ✔

4 2 Caitlin had never felt so scared in her life.
3 The boys not only shouted at her, they also made rude gestures.
4 Young people are hardly ever penalized for breaking the law.

5 2 On no account should vandals be allowed to get away with it.
3 Not since he was cautioned for stealing last year has Richard been in trouble.
4 The police have made no arrests nor do they know who committed the crime. / No arrests have been made. Neither / Nor do the police know who committed the crime.

6 2 Were the plane to be diverted
3 Should you not be happy with the service
4 Were they to require help with their luggage
5 Were I to ask to be upgraded to business class
6 Should you require any assistance

Vocabulary focus

1 1 looking forward to
2 put up with
3 move on to
4 runs out of
5 looks down on
6 goes back on
7 gets away with
8 send off for

2a a come down on
b come up with
c come down with
d come down to
e come up against
f come out in

2b 1 ✔
2 ~~against~~ with
3 ✔
4 ✔
5 ~~out in~~ down with
6 ~~down with~~ out in

3 1 False. You feel strange or ill.
2 Probably true. If you are *off colour*, you feel *slightly ill*.
3 True
4 False. It means you feel tired and not very well.
5 False. If you feel sick the best thing to do is go to the bathroom. It means *want to vomit*. (Although in American English *feel sick* could mean *feel ill*.)
6 True
7 False. You have a *slight* dose.
8 True

Vocabulary expansion

1 1 True
    2 False

2 1 welcomed
    2 spectacles
    3 relish
    4 expiate
    5 innumerable
    6 foresaw
    7 bind
    8 adjusted

3b 1 booming
    2 husky
    3 soothing
    4 grates

4b 1 b
    2 a
    3 d
    4 c

4c 1 glistened
    2 glow
    3 glimmer
    4 glittered / glistened

Listening

1 c

2 1 True
    2 False
    3 False
    4 True

3 1 b
    2 a
    3 b
    4 c

4

●••	●••	•●•
input	logical probably	alliance exciting

•●••	•●•••	••●•
desirable development	inevitable particularly	implications scientific

Language focus

1a 3 ought to
    4 should
    5 don't have to
    6 should
    7 need to
    8 don't have to
    9 had better not
    10 ✔
    11 ✔
    12 B are supposed to
       C don't need to
    13 ✔

2 1 ✔
    2 ~~needn't have taken~~ / didn't need to take
    3 ~~didn't need to study~~ / needn't have studied
    4 ~~needn't have taken~~ / didn't need to take
    5 ~~didn't need to bring~~ / needn't have brought
    6 ✔

3 1 few; every; some
    2 a few
    3 Some
    4 A some / a little
       B any; no
    5 All; some
    6 All; no; every
    7 Little; few / no
    8 a little
    9 Any / Every; some / a little

Vocabulary focus

1 1 injured; injuries
    2 adaptation
    3 description
    4 agreement
    5 nondescript
    6 adaptors
    7 untruth
    8 disagreeable
    9 artistic
    10 basic

Vocabulary expansion

1 1 True
    2 False

2a 1 intake
    2 takeover
    3 take-up
    4 take-off
    5 takeaway

2b 1 takeaway
    2 takeover
    3 take-up
    4 intake

3 1 It could be b but is more likely to be a
    2 c
    3 a
    4 Either a or b
    5 Probably all except garlic, which is a turn-off to some people
    6 b or c
    7 b
    8 b

Listening

1 1 present – the others can all describe natural abilities
    2 identify – the others all mean to help something grow or develop
    3 potentially – the others are all near-synonyms of *very*

2 Students' own answers

3 All except 5

4 1 some area; great athlete; special attention
    2 very particular; encourage
    3 pushy parent
    4 natural ability; directed

5a *receive* attention
    lead a normal childhood
    waste potential
    get pleasure
    achieve a well-rounded personality
    give pleasure

5b 1 the way
2 welcome
3 the joke
4 your breath
5 success
6 a life
7 ten years
8 energy
9 notoriety
10 education

Unit 7

Language focus

1a 1 A I ~~always wanted~~ have always wanted
   B I ~~dyed~~ have dyed
2 A What ~~happened~~ has happened?
   B ~~haven't even known~~ didn't even know
3 A ~~Did you ever have~~ Have you ever had
   B ~~I have first met~~ first met; I ~~have had~~ had; he ~~has looked~~ looked
4 ~~had~~ has had
5 ~~Did Cameron decide~~ Has Cameron decided; he ~~finished~~ has finished

2 1 has spent
2 has returned
3 cycled
4 realized
5 returned
6 began
7 has proved
8 has now covered
9 has seen
10 has sweltered
11 (has) shivered
12 has set up

3 1 been baking
2 touched
3 Both alternatives are possible.
4 been seeing
5 tasted

4 1 A have you been driving
   B passed
   A have been having; have had; did you have
   A didn't pass
2 B I've given up
   A did you stop
   B I haven't had; Have you ever tried
   A I've been meaning

5 1 few
2 minority / few
3 majority
4 Hardly
5 Generally
6 rule

Vocabulary focus

1a 1 view
2 sight
3 sight
4 view
5 sight

1b 1 at first sight
2 in full view
3 came into view
4 out of sight
5 At the sight

2a 1 pop
2 sizzle
3 crack
4 thud
5 screech
6 creak

2b 1 thud
2 sizzling
3 crack
4 screeched
5 creaked
6 popping

3 1 expressed reservations
2 makes sense
3 put in a claim
4 stick to the facts
5 give some thought
6 take my advice

Vocabulary expansion

1a The ideas which are *not* mentioned are: 2, 5, and 8.

2 1 eyes and ears
2 head
3 mouth
4 ear
5 face
6 eyes
7 an eye

3 1 dead-end
2 low-key
3 full-scale
4 high-level
5 hard-core
6 sure-fire
7 split-second

Listening

3 1 They have all had déjà-vu before. One of the women has had it several times.
2 dreams; the mind thinking ahead; past lives

4 First explanation: You dream something before it happens. When it happens you feel that you're re-living it a second time. It's like a premonition.
Second explanation: Your mind thinks ahead to what's going to happen before it does. When it happens you have the sensation that you have experienced it before.

5 1 gripping
2 mind-boggling
3 engrossing
4 intriguing
5 amazing

Unit 8

Language focus

1 2 What some psychologists believe is
3 What they want to do is
4 What parents must remember is
5 What they should not do is

2 1 is the more developed nations which / that
2 we need to do to cut down on the amount of waste we produce is
3 we could all do to improve the situation is
4 (that) it will work is
5 is the amount of packaging that manufacturers use that / which

Answer key   93

3
1 will need to / ~~will be needing to~~ / are going to need to
2 ~~discuss~~ / are going to discuss / will be discussing.
3 ~~will travel~~ / am going to travel / am travelling; ~~will pay~~ / is paying / will be paying
4 will be seeing / ~~are seeing~~ / will see
5 are going to be lost / ~~are being lost~~ / will be lost

4
1 will have finished
2 will be done
3 will make
4 are getting married
5 does … fall
6 is being serviced / is going to be serviced

5
1 ✔
2 ~~will have worked~~ will probably be working
3 ✔
4 Possible but *will have improved* is more likely; ~~will be being reduced~~ / will have been reduced
5 ✔
6 ~~will still have got~~ will still be getting married
7 ~~will be being freed~~ will have been freed
8 ✔ (Also possible: *will study* / *will be studying*)

6
2 will eat / will be eating
3 will have increased
4 will demand / will be demanding
5 will be used
6 will be
7 will encourage
8 will have been reduced
9 will breathe / will be breathing
10 will be regularly replanted / will be replanted regularly

Vocabulary focus

1a
1 True
2 True
3 False. It means that you are not sorry for the crimes you have committed.
4 True
5 False. A petty crime is a small crime like stealing a traffic cone.
6 False. The person is either punished lightly or not at all.
7 Generally false. Although some people who serve a life sentence do spend the rest of their lives in prison, they are in the minority. A life sentence usually means 'a long prison sentence'.

1b
1 (had) turned to crime
2 petty
3 led astray
4 let off
5 hardened
6 fired

Vocabulary expansion

1
1 b
2 d
3 e
4 c
5 a

2a
1 anticlockwise
2 Antiperspirants
3 anti-climax
4 anti-social
5 antiseptic

2b
1 2
2 1
3 2
4 2
5 1

3a
1 d
2 a
3 b
4 c
5 f
6 e

3b
1 post-mortem
2 ad nauseam
3 per annum
4 vice versa
5 per capita

Listening

1
1 They all agree that they should
2 Carole and Anthony: yes; Lisa: enough but not too many
3 Anthony has given his children more freedom than he had. One supposes because of her own experience that Carole would have fewer restrictions and would trust the child to behave in the appropriate way more often. Lisa would bring up her children the same.

2
1 insecure; unloved
2 trust her
3 are given more freedom
4 of social behaviour
5 her own good / benefit

3
1 Not being a parent myself
2 … if they don't have those boundaries they just seem to go a bit crazy …
3 I didn't feel secure …
4 … things I knew I should and shouldn't do …
5 … seemed to be based on my parents not trusting me to behave …
6 … because they assumed I would do something when in fact it never crossed my mind to do that.

Unit 9

Language focus

1
2 … is quite unsatisfactory …
3 You're completely wrong …
4 … felt rather tired …
5 … they're extremely expensive … / I'd absolutely love …
6 … had hardly recovered …
7 … was too difficult …
8 … have scarcely enough …

2
1 I *very much* wanted to go to the concert. / I wanted to go to the concert *very much*.
2 … a *rather interesting* review.
3 ✔
4 The group *had hardly started* playing … / Hardly had the group started playing …
5 The concert was *absolutely perfect*.
6 ✔
7 … but I *rather like* his music.
8 Although it is *quite a* good song …

3
1 Who am I speaking to?
2 things / stuff
3 Because / As I didn't realize …
4 I'd love …
5 I think; got worse; they are building more and more roads.

4
1 disembark; ensure; have all your personal belongings
2 to announce the marriage of their daughter Elizabeth
3 We apologize for not answering / having answered / replying to / having replied to
4 In the event of
5 provided / which are provided

6
1 Time for a reality check
2 from the horses' mouths
3 couple of decent
4 trotted out
5 a few quid
6 moving swiftly on
7 slow things down
8 good luck to them
9 a bit
10 an awful lot of folk out there

Vocabulary focus

1
1 economical
2 classical
3 comic; comical
4 classic
5 economic

2b
1 dependants
2 unsatisfied
3 disinterested
4 misused
5 complement
6 uninterested
7 dissatisfied
8 compliment
9 disuse
10 dependent

Vocabulary expansion

1 1 ★★★★☆

2
1 review
2 tracks
3 lyrical
4 pop music
5 catchy
6 in the charts

3a

Noun	Verb	Adjective
compilation	compile	X
criticism	criticize	(un)critical
simplicity	simplify	simple
universality	X	universal
creativity	create	creative

3b
1 clarification
2 reliability / reliance
3 inability
4 imitation
5 repetition

3c
1 simple
2 repeated
3 imitations
4 creative
5 critical

4a
1 False. It is too complicated to understand.
2 True
3 False. It means nothing out of the ordinary happens.
4 True
5 False. It means modest.
6 True
7 False. It means they are out of one's reach.
8 True

4b
1 uneventful
2 unassuming
3 unflattering
4 unattainable
5 uninspired
6 unfathomable
7 undiminished
8 uncharitable

Listening

1 b

2
1 True
2 False. He thought it was great.
3 True
4 False. Having a drink *and* listening to Frank Sinatra is the best way (according to the speaker).
5 False. It sometimes calms him down or pumps him up.

3
1 c
2 a
3 b
4 a

Unit 10

Language focus

1
1 like
2 as
3 as if
4 Like
5 like; as
6 as

2
1 gets up
2 says
3 walks
4 is playing up
5 adjusts
6 happens
7 lays
8 looks at
9 count out
10 lay
11 am already leaving
12 pull away / am pulling away
13 drips / is dripping

3
1 for putting
2 to see
3 on having
4 you to speak
5 you go
6 on winning
7 for taking
8 to having
9 to sit down
10 using
11 having
12 to take

4 1 forbid you to see
   2 apologize for not telling you
   3 congratulate you on passing
   4 I'd like to thank you / Thank you for
     coming.
   5 insist on speaking
   6 suggest going / we go
   7 advise people to stay

Vocabulary focus

1

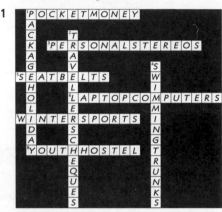

Vocabulary expansion

1 1 To visit the ruins there
   2 Because of the intense heat and
     humidity
   3 b

2a 1 gold
    2 nails
    3 ditchwater
    4 Punch
    5 a sheet
    6 pie
    7 the hills

2b 1 as old as the hills
    2 as white as a sheet
    3 as good as gold
    4 as hard as nails
    5 as easy as pie

3a 1 True
    2 False. You act without thinking about
      the results.
    3 True
    4 False. People would expect the film to
      be boring.
    5 True

3b 1 ominous
    2 treacherous
    3 omnivorous
    4 tedious
    5 impetuous

Listening

1 a

2 1 g
   2 e
   3 a
   4 f
   5 b
   6 d
   7 c

3 1 They had walked there.
   2 The best view was from the 'The Sun
     Gate'
   3 Because it was August – high season.
   4 To be the first to get to the place where
     the best pictures could be taken from.
   5 Horrible. Everyone was pushing and
     shoving people out of the way.
   6 Because he wanted get away from the
     crowds.
   7 He was very glad that he did because he
     was able to enjoy the experience in
     peace.

4 1 e
   2 g
   3 a
   4 b
   5 c
   6 d
   7 f

5 1 wined and dined
   2 shouting and yelling
   3 pick and choose
   4 umming and aahing
   5 cursing and swearing
   6 huffing and puffing

Unit 11

Language focus

1 1 can't have lost
   2 must have bought
   3 B must have been
      A can't have been
      B can / could only have been
   4 can't be / can't have been / can't have
     been being; must be / must have been
     pulling
   5 A can / could he have got to
      B can hardly have forgotten

2 1 b you'd buy if you could afford it?
   2 a Pete recommended we go to?
      b where we celebrated your birthday?
   3 a that / which has the best weather?
      b when most tourists come?
   4 a who said he wouldn't be able to
       come?
      b she is going on holiday with?

3 … in the complex *where* we stayed.
   …, one of *which* had a sea-view.
   My sister Anne, *who* was always car-sick, …
   Our dog, *which* was a German shepherd
   called Honey, …
   … we always stopped at a place *where* we
   could have a barbecue …

4a 1 the
    2 a
    3 An
    4 a
    5 the
    6 a

4b 1 ✔
    2 ~~the~~
    3 ~~the~~
    4 ✔
    5 ✔
    6 ✔
    7 ✔

4c 1 a
    2 A
    3 a
    4 a
    5 a
    6 a
    7 No article
    8 a
    9 the

Vocabulary focus

1 1 back
2 heart
3 reminder
4 memories
5 familiar; ring a bell
6 brain
7 tip
8 blank
9 a sieve; one; the other; jog
10 memorable

2 1 actual
2 arguing
3 remember
4 memories
5 sympathetic
6 date
7 On the other hand
8 present
9 discussing
10 reminds
11 kind
12 souvenirs
13 On the contrary
14 appointment

Vocabulary expansion

1 Memories are made of this.

2 1 aroused
2 raise
3 aroused
4 arisen
5 rose

3 2 readjust
3 recreates / recreated
4 reactivate
5 replaced
6 reaffirmed
7 rearranged
8 redirected

Listening

2 1 Falling over into a paddling pool
2 Three; the speaker, her brother, and her mother

3 1 In the garden.
2 In the paddling pool.
3 Because she fell onto the side of it.
4 She screamed and cried.

4a 1 plonk
2 crawl
3 keel over
4 gush
5 drench
6 gurgle

4b 1 drenching
2 keel over
3 plonked
4 crawled
5 gushed / was gushing
6 gurgled

Unit 12

Language focus

1 3 would load up
4 would be
5 would (finally) get out of
6 would head off
7 would lose
8 would start
9 would pull up / arrive
10 would count up
11 would arrive / pull up
12 would wake up

2 1 ✔
2 ✔
3 am used to eat am used to eating
4 would be used to be
5 A would own owned / used to own
B Would you Did you
6 usen't to be didn't use to be; used you /
did you?
7 ✔
8 didn't use to like ('used not to like' is
sometimes used, but is not very
common)

3 2 Yes, I have lived here long.
3 I will ask John if he'd like to come with
us.
4 I read autobiographies, I read the classics
and I read poetry.
5 I have seen this film many times.

4 1 B *I've got a* headache. *It's* my own fault.
I shouldn't have drunk that wine.

2 A *Is this* yours?

B No *it isn't. It* might be John's.

A *Is this your* watch John?

C *I* wouldn't be seen dead wearing a
watch like that!

3 A *Are you* hungry? *Do you* fancy
something to eat?

B *Are* you offering to cook something?

4 A *It is / was / has been* nice to meet you.

B *It was* nice of you to invite me.

5 A *Have you* read any good books lately?

B *I've read* one or two *good books lately.*
Have you *read any good books lately?*

Vocabulary focus

1 1 sparked off
2 kick off
3 set off
4 blocked off
5 divided off
6 call ... off
7 break off

2 1 leading off
2 put off
3 takes off
4 drive off
5 closed off
6 wave you off
7 rang off

Vocabulary expansion

1 1 c
2 b
3 a

2a 1 b
2 d
3 a
4 c

2b 2 flick; flicked
3 heaves; heave
4 tossed; was tossed; tossed

3a 1 True
2 False. You live in a very remote place.
3 True
4 True, because you are wearing it the wrong way round.
5 False. You constantly criticize the driver (often from the back seat of the car).

3b 1 in the back of beyond
2 back to front
3 put my back up
4 made a comeback
5 back-seat driver

Listening

1 **Speaker 1**   b
Speaker 2   c
Speaker 3   c

2 **Speaker 1**
1 False. He threw him away because he was angry with his mother.
2 False. The expression *to cut off one's nose to spite one's face* means to do something when you are angry with someone else that does at least as much harm to you.

Speaker 2
1 True
2 False. She didn't give them names and she doesn't think that she labelled them either.

Speaker 3
1 False. They took him to the magic shop in town.
2 True

3 **Speaker 1**
mad at
That'll fix you

Speaker 2
kid
I guess
heck

Speaker 3
folks
downtown
heel

Unit 13

Language focus

1 1 looking out
2 reassuring
3 starting
4 wiping
5 shouting
6 reaching
7 leaning / standing
8 distracting
9 standing / leaning
10 floating

2 1 with
2 of
3 at
4 of
5 from
6 with
7 of
8 in

3a 1 of
2 to
3 with
4 in
5 for
6 about
7 on
8 from
9 on
10 from
11 for
12 about

3b 1 blamed Tom for breaking
2 accused Craig of stealing
3 discouraged him from admitting
4 believe in / agree with keeping people
5 is used for draining
6 admitted (to) leaving
7 complain about the train always being
8 stopped him (from) being thrown forward

4 1 ~~are~~ / is
2 ✔
3 ✔
4 has
5 ~~There is~~ / There are
6 ✔
7 ~~are~~ / is
8 ~~have~~ / has
9 ✔
10 ~~has~~ / have
11 ✔
12 ~~has~~ / have

Vocabulary focus

1 1 full-scale
2 resolved
3 bitter
4 fierce
5 blazing
6 reached
7 sparked off
8 pitched
9 quelled
10 won; lost

2a 1 True. They are arguing in a very heated way.
2 False. They think you are making small and unnecessary distinctions in an argument.
3 True
4 True
5 False. You make a conflictive situation better by talking about it openly.
6 False. They find a solution to a disagreement.

2b 1 c
2 d
3 e
4 a
5 b

Vocabulary expansion

1 1 False. They argue about different things. 'This time it's all because of poor Seepie.'
　 2 True
　 3 False. The mother does. She 'has the last word'.

2 1 make
　 2 eyes are
　 3 hand
　 4 fish
　 5 deal
　 6 picture

3 1 good
　 2 put
　 3 breathe
　 4 mince
　 5 In
　 6 go

Listening

1 1 b
　 2 b

2 1 d
　 2 a
　 3 e
　 4 b
　 5 c

3 1 True
　 2 False
　 3 False. She thinks if everyone else can cope, why can't he?
　 4 False. She thinks he should talk to someone.
　 5 True. He doesn't like to say it too directly because the woman is his boss.

4a 1 *you* – weak; *you* – strong; *that* – weak
　 2 *that* – weak; *me* – strong
　 3 *the* – weak; *you* – strong
　 4 *I'm* – strong; *are* – weak; *you* – strong
　 5 *do* – strong; *to* – weak
　 6 *you* – strong; *we're* – weak; *you* – strong

▶ Note • The faster a person speaks the more likely they are to use weak forms. Because the woman speaks more slowly and carefully than the man, she sometimes uses strong forms where another person would use a weak form (sentence 4 – I'm).

　 • We stress the words that we want to emphasize (4 – you; 5 – do)

　 • We generally use the weak forms of the articles *the* and *a*.

　 • Unless *that* is a demonstrative, as in 'that boy', we usually use the weak form.

Unit 14

Language focus

1 1 hasn't succeeded
　 2 can / could
　 3 wasn't able to / couldn't
　 4 could
　 5 couldn't have
　 6 managed to
　 7 cannot / is not able to
　 8 could have / would have been able to
　 9 managed to
　 10 has … succeeded
　 11 have … been able to / will … be able to
　 12 Can; can't
　 13 will be able to / will manage to
　 14 had been able to

2 1 someone
　 2 Everybody; anyone
　 3 Somebody
　 4 Everybody
　 5 anything
　 6 something; someone
　 7 everything; no-one
　 8 anybody
　 9 anyone
　 10 Nobody

3 1 all
　 2 everyone / everybody
　 3 all
　 4 no one / nobody
　 5 everyone / everybody
　 6 all
　 7 no one / nobody

Vocabulary focus

1 1 cohesion
　 2 coincidence
　 3 collocation
　 4 co-operation
　 5 coexistence
　 6 coalition
　 7 collaboration

2 1 shared
　 2 ran / had run
　 3 lock
　 4 cut
　 5 will die
　 6 had gone

Vocabulary expansion

1b 1 more
　 2 more
　 3 more

2a 1 True
　 2 True
　 3 False. You take as long as you need.
　 4 True
　 5 True. But you might change jobs in the future.

2b 1 Not before time
　 2 take your time
　 3 on time
　 4 playing for time
　 5 for the time being

3 1 handy
　 2 terms
　 3 clean
　 4 earth
　 5 crunch

Listening

2 1 Tony would be a surgeon or an electronics engineer (either in computers or telecommunications) because he's interested in machines and how things work.

2 Drawbacks to being a surgeon are the length and expense of training and the responsibility.

3 1 A heart surgeon or an orthopaedic surgeon.

2 He wouldn't choose to be an eye-surgeon because he doesn't like eyes, or a brain surgeon because he doesn't think he is delicate enough.

3 Making mistakes.

4 1 b
2 c
3 a
4 b

5 1 If I really had a choice / then / I'd definitely change / em / and I think there are two possibilities / two things I really would like to do / and which I've always wanted to do …

2 … engineering has always intrigued me / the way things are built / and the way things work / er machines / I love machines / I love tinkering with machines / and in a way the human body is is something like that.

3 You've got all the various systems in the body / and you've got all the various things like the bones / and the various organs / and it would be fascinating I think / trying to repair / this / system.

Unit 15

Language focus

1a … Jack Gibson, *who is* 38 …,
… and his friend Timothy, *who are both* 15 …
The three, *who are* all / *who all come* from Lingdale, Cleveland …

1b Cars *which are* / *have been* fitted …
The cars, *which are* parked …
… vehicles *which are* worth …
… Porsches and Jaguars *which were* / *had been* hidden …

2 … ~~which is~~ in Southend,
found two burglars ~~who were~~ stuck in a lift …
… when people ~~who were~~ leaving a discotheque ~~which is~~ next door …
… Spoils, ~~which is~~ in the High Street …
… the offices, ~~which are~~ above,
…the two men, ~~who are~~ both in their 20s,
… the Club Arts disco, ~~which is~~ next door …

3 2 I usually just have a black coffee for breakfast.
3 I love fried eggs, but I loathe scrambled eggs.
4 The cathedral stands in the centre of the old part of the town.
5 I absolutely detest shopping on a Saturday afternoon.
6 I wouldn't have guessed the answer in a million years.
7 I never imagined she wasn't telling the truth.
8 I find driving in the dark difficult.

4 2 to take
3 ✔
4 cheating
5 ✔
6 being found out
7 ✔
8 being over

5 1 to tell
2 offering
3 getting
4 spending
5 to have
6 to inform
7 to tell
8 making
9 to post
10 A to lose; having
B joining

6 1 going / driving
2 barking / whining / howling
3 shout
4 bang / slam
5 open
6 leave
7 get out
8 put
9 looking

Vocabulary focus

1a

greater or better than	separate from; isolated	showing shock or disapproval
outgrow	outback	outrageous
outdo	outbuildings	outlandish
outwit	outsiders	

1b 1 outrageously
2 outgrown
3 Outsiders
4 outwit
5 outdid
6 outlandish
7 outbuildings

Vocabulary expansion

2 Because they like to have secrets and know things other people don't.

3a 1 True
2 False. You find out information about someone by secretly listening in to their conversation.
3 False. You hide it from people.
4 False. They are deceiving you.
5 True
6 True

3b 1 eavesdropping
2 conceal
3 misleading
4 leading her on
5 collude
6 led her up the garden path

4b 1 giggled
2 chuckling
3 cackled
4 tittered
5 sniggered

Listening

1 b

3 1 b
   2 b
   3 a
   4 b
   5 a

4a 1 b
   2 c
   3 d
   4 a

4b 1 in retrospect / looking back
   2 feel sorry for / sympathize with
   3 happened to
   4 There's no way

Unit 16

Language focus

1 2 will make / fix
   3 always set
   4 will lie / sleep
   5 not to go
   6 will get / have
   7 nod / doze / drop
   8 am having
   9 to lie

2 1 This application form has to be seen to be believed. It has been filled in
   2 The name of the new chair will probably be announced
   3 This was not the first time his application had been turned down.
   4 No one has been appointed to Mr Jones' old post since he was promoted last month.
   5 Interviews are going to be held next week.
   6 Candidates are asked to send in
   7 Successful applicants will be required
   8 I'm sure John wouldn't have been turned down
   9 No one with a degree could be expected
   10 Your application must either be typed or word-processed.

3 1 was set
   2 grows / grew
   3 compiled
   4 has been eaten
   5 are cherished
   6 is used
   7 is cut down
   8 polished up
   9 consists
   10 has been used
   11 is grown
   12 to be taken
   13 reproduces

4 1 her to apply
   2 you to see
   3 him to listen
   4 him to take
   5 her to swim
   6 you to ride

5 1 invited / has invited us to go
   2 advised me / him / her to try
   3 caused the car to skid
   4 expect me to be / arrive
   5 can't bear you to see
   6 would prefer you to do
   7 persuaded Patrick to go

6 1 on me having
   2 I went
   3 from smoking
   4 getting
   5 do
   6 stay
   7 to wear
   8 to introduce

Vocabulary focus

1a

verb	noun	noun (person)
apply	application	applicant
X	candidature candidacy	candidate
employ	employment	employer employee
graduate	graduation	graduate
interview	interview	interviewer interviewee
qualify	qualifications	X
refer	reference	referee

1b 1 employment; employers
   2 applicants / applications
   3 interviewers
   4 graduates
   5 referees

Vocabulary expansion

1b 1 about 2 p.m.
   2 just before you go to bed
   3 won't
   4 will
   5 cool
   6 more

2a 1 soothing
   2 appetizing
   3 intoxicating
   4 invigorating
   5 stimulating
   6 refreshing

2b 1 intoxicating
   2 invigorating
   3 refreshing
   4 appetizing
   5 soothing
   6 stimulating

3a 1 True
   2 False. It means you have a new idea, but it could be anywhere.
   3 False. It means they do not take an active part in the management. Instead they usually provide money at the outset.
   4 True
   5 True
   6 False. It means they think you have no chance at all.
   7 False. You daydream (= think of pleasant things when you should be concentrating on something else) when you are awake.
   8 True

3b 1 daydreaming
   2 sleep in
   3 slept like a log
   4 sleep on it
   5 Sweet dreams
   6 Dream on!

Listening

2 1 Yes she does.

2 Stress, pressure, life changes

3 1 False. The dream is about being away with her family.

2 True

3 False. She wakes up before the plane leaves.

4 True

5 False. She thinks she knows.

4 1 True

2 False. They want you to hurry.

3 False. They annoy you.

4 False. You start working seriously on something.

5 True

Unit 17

Language focus

1 1 with

2 about

3 about

4 of

5 for

6 to; for

7 with

8 for

9 A to   B for

10 A with   B at; for

2 1 depend on

2 criticized for / accused of

3 aimed at

4 objected to

5 apply for

6 accused of / criticized for

7 resort to

8 congratulated … on

3 1 It

2 Both

3 They

4 The former

5 The latter

6 These

4a 1 his

2 those

3 whose

4 they

5 What

6 It

7 It

8 That

4b 2 the London critics

3 the Angel's

4 the wings

5 hearing the Angel described as brash and meaningless

6 the criticism

7 the form

8 making a plaster mould of himself first

Vocabulary focus

1b 1 man-made – artificial

2 Barmaids and barmen – bar staff

3 headmaster – head teacher / head

4 policemen – police officers

5 undermanned – understaffed

6 a man – someone / an engineer, etc

7 No man – Nobody / no person

8 Air-hostesses – flight attendants

9 Mankind – The human race is / Humankind is / Human beings are

10 wives – partners

Vocabulary expansion

1 The trouble with women who do too much

2a 1 for

2 into

3 with

4 at

2b 1 greatly

2 hard; heavy

3 Both possible

2c 1 having a go at

2 highly / sharply critical

3 constructive

4 fierce / severe / widespread criticism

3 1 form

2 course

3 mill

4 risk

5 family

6 riot

Listening

1 **Recording 1**

1 b

2 Yes

3 b

Recording 2

1 c

2 Yes

3 c

2 **Recording 1**

1 False. According to the speaker, they have only heard of the cows.

2 False. They feel ashamed of it.

3 True

4 True

Recording 2

1 False. It's an area of the old city.

2 True

3 False. There was a building behind the piece that had coloured glass in the walls.

4 False

3 2 this is a

3 a town that is quite

4 for one of its particular works of public art

5 very few people have actually seen them

6 everybody's heard of them

7 How are the concrete cows?

8 the residents of the town

9 a source of

10 of shame and embarrassment

Unit 18

Language focus

1 2 They had to grow their own food or they would starve.
3 They were allowed to keep farm animals such as cows so they had a source of milk.
4 They didn't sleep in ordinary houses but in special 'pods'.
5 People found it a difficult experience yet they would not have missed it for the world.

2 1 We could reduce crime by denying criminals
2 People who are desperate for fame will do anything
3 If we refused to use the names of criminals (then)
4 Hoping to be remembered, a young man in ancient Greece
5 Although a criminal may achieve overnight fame,

3 1 get your eyes tested.
2 All his windows got broken / He got all his windows broken
3 to get lost
4 got it back.
5 get this work done / finished
6 get unpacked; get changed

4a 1 by
2 up to
3 of
4 on
5 round
6 at

4b 1 getting at
2 getting up to
3 get out of
4 get round to
5 get by
6 get on

Vocabulary focus

1 2 notoriety
3 glory
4 renown
5 heroism
6 celebrities
7 famous / famed
8 reputation

Vocabulary expansion

1 1 On an island in a national park in Thailand.
2 Because they think it will be unspoiled by tourists.

2a 1 b
2 e
3 a
4 f
5 c
6 d

2b 1 licked her lips
2 stamping your foot
3 drummed her fingers
4 shrugged her shoulders
5 raised her eyebrows
6 wrinkled up his nose

3 1 scoured
2 ransacked
3 searched
4 been through
5 seeks
6 rummaged about

Listening

2 1 Yes
2 The cinema, newspapers, spontaneity (not having to plan things in advance), cafés
3 urban transport and traffic jams

3 1 So she could spend time doing her own thing.
2 Having to plan ages in advance if you wanted to meet people.
3 The noise and the energy.
4 Having to justify every minute of her time.
5 Small urban problems that are really unimportant.
6 Sitting in traffic jams.

4 1 doing your own thing
2 justify
3 babble
4 cut-throat
5 get het up about something

5 1 b
2 a
3 b
4 a

OXFORD
UNIVERSITY PRESS

Great Clarendon Street, Oxford OX2 6DP

Oxford University Press is a department of the University of Oxford.
It furthers the University's objective of excellence in research, scholarship, and education by publishing worldwide in

Oxford New York

Auckland Bangkok Buenos Aires Cape Town Chennai Dar es Salaam Delhi Hong Kong Istanbul Karachi Kolkata Kuala Lumpur Madrid Melbourne Mexico City Mumbai Nairobi São Paulo Shanghai Taipei Tokyo Toronto

Oxford and Oxford English are registered trade marks of Oxford University Press in the UK and in certain other countries

© Oxford University Press 2002

Database right Oxford University Press (maker)

First published 2002
Second impression 2003

No unauthorized photocopying

All rights reserved. No part of this publication may be reproduced, stored in a retrieval system, or transmitted, in any form or by any means, without the prior permission in writing of Oxford University Press, or as expressly permitted by law, or under terms agreed with the appropriate reprographics rights organization. Enquiries concerning reproduction outside the scope of the above should be sent to the ELT Rights Department, Oxford University Press, at the address above

You must not circulate this book in any other binding or cover and you must impose this same condition on any acquirer

Any web sites referred to in this publication are in the public domain and their addresses are provided by Oxford University Press for information only. Oxford University Press disclaims any responsibility for the content.

Designed by Stephen Strong

ISBN 0 19 4379612

Printed in Spain by Unigraf Artes Gráficas, S.L.

The author and publisher are grateful to those who have given permission to reproduce the following extracts and adaptations of copyright material:

p.11 Extract from 'Long Live the Queen' by Ruth Rendell, *Good Housekeeping* December 1991. Reproduced by permission of Peters, Fraser & Dunlop on behalf of Kingsmarkham Enterprises Ltd.

p.12 'Is big brother watching you?' by Nick Paton-Walsh © *The Guardian* 18 July 1999. Reproduced by permission of Guardian Newspapers Ltd.

p.15 'The complete guide to your future' by Simon Reeve, *Focus Magazine* October 1998 © National Magazine Company. Reproduced by permission.

p.16 Extract from *Savage Skies*. Reproduced by permission of Granada Media.

p.20 Extract from *999 Dramatic Stories of Real-Life Rescues* by Michael Buerk © Michael Buerk. Reproduced by permission of BBC Worldwide Ltd.

p.21 'Traffic chaos as heath blaze shuts motorway' © 1996 The Surrey Advertiser. Reproduced by permission.

p.26 Extract from *The Edible Woman* by Margaret Atwood. Reproduced by permission of Andre Deutsch Ltd.

p.29 'Top of the class' by Peter Kingston © *The Guardian* 21 October 1997. Reproduced by permission of Guardian Newspapers Ltd.

pp.32&33 'Around the world on a bike' by Sarah Barnett, *Focus Magazine* June 2000 © National Magazine Company. Reproduced by permission.

p.38 'Happy New Year…2022 that is!' by Sarah Gibbings, *Woman* 6 January 1992. Reproduced by permission of IPC Media Ltd.

p.42 'CD Review: The Corrs' by Chris Charles, *BBC News Online* 16 July 2000. Reproduced by permission of BBC News Online.

p.44 'CD Review: The Beatles' by Darren Waters, *BBC News Online* 13 November 2000. Reproduced by permission of BBC News Online.

p.46 Extract from *Every Dead Thing* by John Connolly. Reproduced by permission of Hodder and Stoughton Ltd.

p.48 Extract from *Nothing to Declare* by Mary Morris © Mary Morris 1998. Reproduced by permission of Houghton Mifflin Company. All rights reserved.

p.51 'Swedes find it pays to put up with ads on the phone' by Jon Henley © *The Guardian* 21 January 1997. Reproduced by permission of Guardian Newspapers Ltd.

p.52 'Smell not to be sniffed at as memory clue' by Libby Brooks © *The Guardian* 11 February 1999. Reproduced by permission of Guardian Newspapers Ltd.

p.54 Extract from *Places in the Heart* by Susan Kurosawa (1997). Reprinted by permission of Hodder Headline.

p.56 'What a comeback' by Vicki Reeve, *Evening Standard Magazine* 7 July 2000. Reproduced by permission of Solo Syndication Ltd.

p.58 Extract from *The Tesseract* by Alex Garland © Alex Garland 1996. Reproduced by permission of Penguin Group (UK).

p.61 Extract from *Dance With a Poor Man's Daughter* by Pamela Jooste © Pamela Jooste. Reproduced by permission of Transworld Publishers, a division of the Random House Group Ltd. All rights reserved.

p.64 Extract from *The Breath of Angels* by John Beattie. Reproduced by permission of Mainstream Publishing, www.mainstreampublishing.com.

p.65 'The time squeeze' by Helen Wilkinson and Geoff Mulgan, *The Guardian* 6 June 1995. Reproduced by permission of Demos Quarterly.

p.67 'Stormy cruise ends happily', *Daily Express* March 1990. Reproduced by permission of Express Newspapers Ltd.

p.67 'Bug beating car thieves', *Daily Express* 17 September 1994. Reproduced by permission of Express Newspapers Ltd.

p.67 'Bungling burglars let down by overloaded lift' by Robin Young © Times Newspapers Ltd, 26 December 1994. Reproduced by permission.

p.69 Extract from *Daddy We Hardly Knew You* by Germaine Greer. Reproduced by permission of Penguin Group (UK).

p.77 'Heaven sent' by Stephen Goodwin, *The Independent* 28 February 1998. Reproduced by permission of Independent Newspapers (UK) Ltd.

p.78 'The trouble with women who do too much' by Angela Lambert, *The Independent* 1 July 1995. Reproduced by permission of Independent Newspapers (UK) Ltd.

p.82 Extract from *The Beach* by Alex Garland © Alex Garland 1998. Reproduced by permission of Penguin Group (UK).

Although every effort has been made to trace and contact copyright holders before publication, this has not been possible in some cases. We apologize for any apparent infringement of copyright and if notified, the publisher will be pleased to rectify any errors or omissions at the earliest opportunity.

The publisher would also like to thank the following for permission to reproduce photographs:

Action-Plus p.36; AKG London p.43; Axiom Photographic Agency pp.79 (D.Young/cows by fence), (C.Martin/people with bull), (T.Adamson/bull with Bilbao writing); Corbis pp.6 (D.S.Robbins), 49 (G.Powell), 52 (Bettmann), 67, (Travel Ink/two men on scaffolding), (Kelly–Mooney Photography/scaffolding on building); Frank Spooner Pictures pp.32 & 33 © Heinz Stücke; Getty Images/Image Bank p.17 (A.Gallant), 53 (T.Radigonda), 73 (Infocus), 77 (A.Edwards); Getty Images/Stone pp.15 (ESA/K.Horgan), 18 (C.Wahlberg), 23 (M.Rutz), 30 (P.Ingrand), 39 (T.MacPherson), 48 (C.Krebs), 62 (F.Herholdt), 66 (C.Widsor/shopkeeper), (M.Rosenfeld/car mechanic), 72 (S.Westmorland/forest), 76 (J.Millar), 79 (D.E.Cox/fist sculpture), (R.Passmore/abstract sculpture); Getty Images/Telegraph pp.10 (A.Mo), 20 (VCL/S.Powell), 24 (A.Smith), 31 (T.Andersen), 37 (M.Krasowitz), 65 (K.Laubacher), 66 (Chabruken/woman at drawing table), (M.S.Salmeron/surveyor with hard hat); Hulton Archive pp.57 (1970s), 78 (Lady Hester Stanhope on horseback); 79 (P.Stanley/figures and window); PA Photos pp.57 (21st century/ABACA Press), 78 (C.Ison/yachtswoman Ellen MacArthur); PhotoDisc pp.7 (traveller), 16 (raindrop & cloud), 21, 27, 29 (man & boy), 34, 47, 82; Pictorial Press pp.8, 44 (1967), 81, 82 (Di Caprio with spear); Rex Features pp.7 (phone box), 19 (H.Evans), 35 (D.Stone), 42 (B.Basic), 44 (1964); Science Photo Library pp.66 (M.Donne/surgeon), (G.Tompkinson/scientist with microscope), 72 (P.Goetgheluck/bamboo stem cut through); Still Moving Picture Company p.16 (A.Johnston/wedding); Sygma p.60

Illustrations by:
Stefan Chabluk p.21; Paul Dickinson p.46; Emma Dodd pp.8, 15, 20, 33, 37, 51, 59, 61, 71, 75; Ian Jackson pp.10, 17, 25, 41, 50, 52, 63, 83; Marie-Hélène Jeeves pp.14, 28, 38, 55, 56, 80, 81; Ian Miller p.54; Mark Olroyd p.26; Susan Scott pp.11, 64; Guy Passey p.58; Paul Young p.68